In the French Kitchen Garden

In the French Kitchen Garden

The Joys of Cultivating a Potager

Georgeanne Brennan

Illustrations by Melissa Sweet

CHRONICLE BOOKS
SAN FRANCISCO

Library of Congress Cataloging-in Publication Data:
Brennan, Georgeanne, 1943-
    In the french kitchen garden : the joys of cultivating a potager / by Georgeanne Brennan.
    p. cm.
    Includes index.
    ISBN 0-8118-2034-3 (hc)
    1.Vegetable gardening. 2. Herb gardening. 3. Cookery (Vegetables). 4. Cookery (Herbs)
I. Title.
SB321.B74   1998
635—dc21   97-50335
                CIP

Printed in Hong Kong.
Edited by Sharon Silva
Designed and composed by Gretchen Scoble

Distributed in Canada by Raincoast Books
8680 Cambie Street
Vancouver, British Columbia V6P 6M9

10 9 8 7 6 5 4 3 2 1

Chronicle Books
85 Second Street
San Francisco, California 94105

Web Site: www.chronbooks.com

Table of Contents

ACKNOWLEDGMENTS

Thank you to the people who have shared
with me their love of gardening, food, and the good life,
beginning with my late mother, who was an intuitive gardener,
an adventuresome cook, and a lover of good food
at a table well set. To my husband, Jim,
who continues to be an enthusiastic partner with me
in life's projects, large and small.
To Marcel and Marie Palazolli and M. and Mme Lamy,
who have let me work alongside them in potagers, fields,
and kitchens, and who have shared so many meals
with me over many years.
To all the Fines, who continue to inspire me as much today
as they did twenty-five years ago when I first met them in France.
To Charlotte Kimball, my partner in Le Marché Seeds
and longtime friend, who shared not only her knowledge
but many adventures and discoveries as well.
To Donald Brennan, with whom I first began my life in France,
and to my children, who are so much a part of
life's pleasures.

To my husband,

Jim

INTRODUCTION

A POTAGER, OR FRENCH-STYLE KITCHEN GARDEN, IS DIFFERENT from the classic American harvest garden, which is planted in spring and culminates in late summer, with much of the harvest preserved for winter's use. A potager is a year-round garden whose purpose is to supply the kitchen on a daily basis with fresh vegetables and herbs. It is cyclical not linear, because even while being harvested in the current season, it is continually being replanted for the coming season. Potagers are an integral part of the French food tradition, and although their numbers are diminishing, a trip through France will reveal plots of land planted to vegetables in front of houses, along streambeds and railroad tracks, and behind blocks of urban flats. Some sport toolsheds, overstuffed chairs, scarecrows, or decorative walls, and almost all are planted in a personalized fashion.

Potagers are part of the French patrimony, found on grand estates and behind humble farmhouses. Having fresh food with which to cook every day has long been a national imperative in France, and French regional cooking, *cuisine du terroir,* derives its individual character from the products of the local potagers and the specialties of the area—the local cheeses, fruits, and nuts, the fish and wild game. Thus cabbages harvested from potagers in the Berry, a region south of Paris notable for its wild game, may become part of a slowly braised dish made with pheasants and chestnuts, while a cabbage cut in the eastern region of Alsace finds its finest expression in a *choucroute garni.*

Literally "soup garden," a potager is classically composed of vegetables, strawberries, melons, a few annual herbs, and perhaps some simple cutting flowers, such as zinnias and nasturtiums. Properly speaking, fruit trees belong not in the potager but in the *verger*, or home orchard. As with many things, however, rules are broken, and a single fruit tree, such as a fig or peach, is often found in the kitchen garden. The herb garden contains the perennials thyme, oregano, marjoram, tarragon, and rosemary and is planted elsewhere as well, but the most popular annual herbs, basil, chervil, and cilantro, have a place in the potager, as does the perennial parsley.

Generally only large enough to provide food for the family on a daily basis, a potager commonly yields only a few vegetables for preserving, but part of the harvest, such as potatoes, onions, and winter squashes, is stored in cool caves, or cellars, to be used as needed. A family of four might require a space of only nine feet by twelve feet to provide leeks, tomatoes, beans, herbs, cabbages, radishes, and lettuces on a seasonal basis. An extended family, including grandparents, grown children, their spouses, and children, sharing a potager, as they often do in France, would have a piece of land several times larger.

Certainly there is nothing new about planting a vegetable garden, and this book is not so much about how to grow vegetables—how deep to plant the seeds, how much fertilizer to apply, how to treat specific diseases or ward off particular insects—as it is about a style of gardening. The French-style kitchen garden, time-honored and deeply ingrained in the culture, is nevertheless immensely practical and adaptable for today's busy Americans. Most residents of the United States now live in suburban or urban settings, but even suburban houses generally have yards, front, side, and back, where a small section can be allocated to a potager. City dwellers have more limited space, but since a potager can be grown in containers on a balcony, rooftop, or fire escape, or in a small area of a shared backyard, they, like their French counterparts, can revel in freshly grown herbs and vegetables. Many American cities have begun to allocate municipally owned land for use as vegetable gardens, a long-standing practice in France. A wonderful camaraderie among the gardeners results, engendered by shared experiences and the learning together from failures and successes.

Unlike the French, Italians, English, and other Europeans, Americans do not have a tradition of year-round kitchen gardens. But that doesn't mean that we can't grow them. I am a passionate believer in potagers and their worth both in the kitchen and to the spirit, but over the years whenever I have espoused them, the rejoinder is always, "Yes, you can grow one because you live in California. But what about people who don't? What about the Midwest or the Northeast, or even the South, places with winter snows and freezes?" I reply that where a harsh continental climate prevails in areas of France, Italy, Russia, Germany, and England, I have seen snow-covered potagers in December and January, with cabbages and kale peeking through and with sweet, red radicchio heads protected under layers of mulch. In all but the most severe climates—those where winter temperatures drop far below freezing and stay there for days, where the ground is a solid icy block— a year-round garden can be grown. Granted, it requires extra measures on the part of the gardener to produce vegetables throughout the seasons, or nearly so, in regions with bitter cold winters, but careful selection of winter-hardy varieties will increase success, just as does the selection of heat-tolerant varieties for regions with very hot summers.

Success with a year-round garden can also be increased by an understanding of the seasons and of the seasonality of the vegetables we eat, no matter where we live. Spring comes to all of us, albeit at different times, and subtle indicators of its arrival are common for all. For example, one is the blossoming of fruit trees, which begins when temperatures reach a certain level and the sap in the trees begins to flow as dormancy ends. This may occur anytime between February and May, depending upon where they are growing.

No matter where a potager is tended, its elements remain the same. The various parts of the garden are divided into plots that are individually rotational. Year-round daily harvest requires planning and management, a knowledge of the local seasons, and of the seasonality of the vegetables and herbs themselves.

A potager can be started in spring, summer, or early fall, once the ground has been prepared. The initial planting will take about two-thirds of the prepared ground, with the remaining one-third to be planted later and harvested in the next season. For example, a potager begun in early spring will have a full flush of tender lettuces when it is time to put in summer squashes and beans, so some space needs to be left open to plant for an ongoing harvest. If the garden is started in early summer, it might be planted with eggplants, tomatoes, and peppers, leaving space to plant the fall-harvest vegetables later. A potager begun in late summer or early fall would be replete with lettuces, spinach, radishes, and other quick-growing crops, with space left open for a late winter or very early spring planting of onions, garlic, and carrots. As each crop finishes its harvest, its space is cleared, the ground is turned, and something else planted for harvest the following season. The initial challenge is not the growing of the vegetables. Instead, it is the management and planning that justifies removing a vegetable or herb that is still edible but on the wane in order to sow for the next season. Only then is the garden always full of the best of the season.

We all agree that there are four seasons—spring, summer, fall, and winter—and that each one evidences certain characteristics in varying degrees. But not only do the characteristics vary from region to region, so, too, do the arrival and length of the seasons themselves. Where I live in northern California, spring arrives in February, announced by blossoms and new leaves covering the trees and the blooming of the daffodils and tulips. Yet it is still winter in New York City, where the branches are bare and the daffodils and tulips only green shoots. So, rather than try to estimate planting dates for the many diverse growing regions of the country and attempt to account for microclimates and their variations, I have instead included a section on seasons and seasonality that will serve as a guide to learning about one's own particular seasons and when to plant.

The book is organized into five chapters. The first, Creating a Personal Potager, contains general information about selecting a site and soil, water, and sunlight needs, and discusses container planting, soil mixes, and some design ideas. This chapter also offers directions on preparing the ground, some planting techniques, and a section on seasonality. The remainder of the book is divided into chapters devoted to the individual seasons. Because the division between seasons is fluid rather than precise, each chapter is preceded by a short essay on the garden in transition, that period when one season's vegetables are in their final flush, while the next season's vegetables are just beginning to produce. The summer chapter is unique because it has a section devoted to summer planting for fall and winter harvest, as that is when some of the plantings for those seasons must occur in order to ensure a harvest. The chapters themselves open with a brief overview of what to do in the garden during that season, followed by vegetables to plant and relevant potager gardening techniques, often illustrated with my own observations and experiences in potagers over the years, both here and in France. Since fresh vegetables and herbs are the *raison d'être* of a potager, recipe ideas for seasonal fare are interspersed throughout the chapters.

My purpose in writing this book is to inspire others to plant a potager, to grow their own vegetables and herbs for their own kitchen on a daily basis, even if only one or two different things each season, and to learn from their successes and failures, as all gardeners do. It is the learning, along with the harvests, over the years and through the seasons, that brings the greatest pleasure, as the rhythms of the seasons and their bounty become internalized. Thus not only is a bowl of freshly pulled radishes, accompanied by sweet butter and fresh bread, a fine way to start a spring meal, but their planting, growth, pulling, and preparation serve as a memory trigger for springs past—not just the memory of the garden but of all that occurs in the seasons of our lives.

When I first planted a potager, not in France where we had been living, but in the front yard of our small house in a quiet California town, I didn't know that having a year-round kitchen garden would become an imperative, as important to my well-being as fresh air, red wine, and the warmth of the winter sun.

In 1970, my husband and I and another couple had purchased an old stone farmhouse in southern France and bought goats to start a small

S	M	T	W	T	F	S
				2	3	4
5	6	7	8	9	10	11
12	13	14	15	16	17	18
19	20	21	22	23	24	25
26	27	28	29	30		

SEED	DAYS ···→ GERMINATION	MOON	PLANTING DATE
CHARD	*fifty seven*	☽	3·23
LETTUCE:			3·30
CARDINALE	six ty		
MESCLUN	six ty		
MERVEILLE des QUATRE SAISONS	58 - 61		
	(early)	D	4·3
PEAS: CADICE	*fifty-five*		

CLOCHE LETTUCES

cheese-making business. The shared living adventure did not work well, and so my husband and I rented other places temporarily, keeping the goats. At these various houses, for one reason or another, we had no kitchen garden, although I longed for one. The neighbors were always kind, however, and would often give us tomatoes, fava beans, melons, and lettuce from their patches according to season and abundance.

A potager came with our fourth and final house. It said so on the deed, which also designated a threshing ground, the rights to a deep well, a stable, two hay lofts, a pigeon tower, a barn, and a small *cabanon des outils,* or tool-shed. The tile roof of the toolshed had fallen in and the wall had a dangerous crack. The four-story-tall pigeon tower had tumbled eight or nine years before, blocking the entrance to the stable. Thus, to reach the larger of the two lofts, it was necessary to pass through a neighbor's loft and then enter through a four-foot-high door that was usually blocked with hay. The small barn was still intact, so we kept the goats there for the last season before we returned to California. The threshing ground, of which we owned a third, had become a vast grass-covered field where visiting children played chase and soccer, its expanse marred only by the ruts of a tractor road leading to the vineyards beyond.

At the far end of the threshing ground and up a rise, next to the deep well, was the potager, covered with artichokes, strawberries, tomatoes, peppers, and eggplants. Maurice Luchesi had kept a year-round kitchen garden there for over thirty years, practically from the time he first arrived as a ten-year-old orphan to work on the farm of M. and Mme Isnard.

We first met Maurice and his wife, Françoise, when we rented a small, rabbity house belonging to Victorine and Michel Freinet. Michel was the local schoolteacher, and in their spare time he, Victorine, and their teenaged sons, Robert and Paul, were building a house from the ruins of a tile factory.

Three stone rooms of our little house had originally been vats, waist high but large enough and high enough to hold the clay from which the tiles were made and with doorways no wider than my hips. This had been the first construction project for the Freinets, and here they lived until the main house was habitable. Up the road from the Freinets was the home of Maurice and Françoise. At that time they were tenant farmers and, although among the poorest people in the region, were known for their kindness and generosity. Long before we bought our rambling collection of stone walls and roofs and became permanent neighbors, Maurice and Françoise kept our small family well supplied with whatever grew in their potager. Our daughters were the same age, and my daughter, Ethel, and I would often join Françoise and her daughter, Aileen, on walks to their potager, where I would help with harvesting while we talked, always coming home with a full basket.

After we purchased the property, Maurice continued to maintain the potager and we helped ourselves. The arrangement was wonderfully convenient. We hadn't the skills, tools, or time to devote to a garden then, while for Maurice it was a labor of love, something to do after his long day in the fields. He has always preferred vegetables to vineyards. A short six months after we signed the first papers for the property, and having moved only the goats, we unexpectedly decided to return to California after the sudden death of my father-in-law. Who knew when we would be back again? It was only natural for Maurice to continue to grow vegetables in our potager, as indeed he still does, although now, decades later, he is no longer a tenant farmer but a landowner in his own right.

In the meantime, back in northern California where my husband had taken a teaching job, we planted our front-yard potager. Much of the seed we sowed, including fava beans and Charentais melons, had been sent to us by our French friends. We added the American favorites of corn and okra, as well as some French cornichons purchased by mail.

Our yard was small, only about two hundred square feet, and divided nearly in half by a walkway leading to the front porch. A rented rototiller supplied the muscle to turn over the sod of half the yard, which seemed to be mostly Bermuda grass. Raked and cleared of roots, the soil was beautiful, dark and sweet smelling. We sectioned the dug half into five beds for squashes, melons, cucumbers, radishes, and lettuces. Then we made rows for beans, tomatoes, eggplants, peppers, the corn and okra, a patch for a few pumpkin plants, and added a smattering of cosmos and zinnias for color and cutting.

After the first marauding dog chased our cat across the careful plantings, we surrounded the yard with a four-foot-high chicken-wire fence, running it right across the dividing walk-way, and used the driveway instead to reach the front porch.

In the warm spring weather of California's Central Valley, helped by our careful watering, the little front yard was soon alive with hundreds of sprouts. Our children, then seven and three, were both entranced by what was happening. They had little watering cans and trowels, and when picking time neared for the first vegetables, they equipped themselves with baskets and boxes for bringing in the harvest.

Summer came and the days turned hotter and hotter. I developed an early morning ritual of taking my coffee cup into the cool garden, where I inspected each plant, pondered what to cook for dinner, and reveled in a peaceful interlude between waking and the day beginning. Worries drifted away. I forgot about myself, lost in the world of plants, earth, and insects. Later, after a second cup of coffee, I would do any watering or weeding needed, and, of course, have a morning harvest. In the evening the ritual was repeated, the coffee replaced with a glass of wine or lemonade.

As summer drew to an end, though, so did the garden. The corn was spent and the tomato and cucumber vines nearly barren. I wanted the garden to continue, so I could have vegetables the year around, like Maurice and Françoise and our other French friends. We took out the straggling summer plants, leaving only a last tomato plant or two, the pumpkin plant, and the herbs. Turning over the remaining ground, we dug in rotted steer and chicken manure from the high-school farm where my husband taught animal husbandry. Once again, we were ready to plant. That fall and winter, we feasted on cabbage, broccoli, cauliflower, lettuces, leeks, and greens. When early spring came, in went radishes, new lettuces, and turnips. But that summer, after a year of two teachers' salaries, we returned to France for the first time since leaving. It had been four years.

Friends had done some work on our house to make it more habitable, although we still had no running water or electricity. Maurice kept us well supplied in melons from his fields and peaches and plums from his orchard, and we helped ourselves to whatever was growing in the potager. I would set out for the garden each morning with my basket over my arm to gather what I needed for lunch and again in the late afternoon or evening to provide for dinner. Sometimes the children went with me, but more often than not they were tossing balls on the old threshing ground, or playing hide-and-seek in the vineyards at the forest's edge, or simply sitting on the cool stone steps, inventing games and stories.

Today, the children are grown, their father and I are divorced, and the memories of those lazy summers together in France are bittersweet for us all. The children and I have continued to go back to the house together, sometimes with their friends or stepbrothers, building new memories. My husband of twelve years and I go together, usually in late fall or winter, and he has become, I think, as enamored of the life there as I have always been. Often he'll ask if he should go out to the potager and get some greens for salad or a few leeks for soup. The ritual of the quiet walk across the old threshing ground, with the forest and mountains looming to the west where the vineyards end, lures him as it does me.

One of the first things I did when we bought the house and small farm where we live now in northern California, even before we moved in, was to plant a potager. It was small and very jumbly. I had a patch of alpine strawberries, one of thyme, some potatoes, parsley, and later tomatoes, peppers, eggplant, and basil. During those traumatic early years of divorce and a new husband, the potager became my source of solace. When down in spirit, I would find myself in my garden. Soon I would be distracted, noticing how many new strawberries we had, freeing the tomato seedlings from encroaching pigweed, and filling my pockets with thyme, thinking about stuffing a chicken with it for dinner.

Since the first effort, we've had a potager almost continuously, although its makeup often varies, depending upon our planning and management. Some years we have had a magnificent winter potager with row upon orderly row filled with different radicchios, escarole, cabbages, parsley, chervil,

Italian Lacinato kale, and Chinese greens. Other years we've managed only a few radicchio plants and some parsley. In a well-planned spring, the potager has been an evolving patchwork of bright greens and reds, sporting radishes, baby turnips, and fluffy carrot tops, and red romaine, red oakleaf, and Batavian lettuces with stately rows of young leeks, onions, and garlic outlining its perimeter. Some summers we have had dozens of tomato plants, eggplants, and peppers, arranged in rows and patches, intermingled with towers of haricots verts, rounds of squash plants bounded by rows of Charentais melons, and lush carpets of different basils. Other years have seen only a few tomatoes and a little basil. Whether abundant or spare, my kitchen garden always offers me daily food and a respite from life, a place where I know that once there, I will be caught up by the thrill of what is growing, what more I could plant, and what I will cook that day or the next or the next.

The planting space changes somewhat from year to year, and the area where we put in our first garden is now covered with irises and roses. For the last six years, though, I have luxuriated in a definite potager within the perimeter of an old-fashioned scalloped-wire fence, erected ostensibly to keep out the rabbits. The rabbits have come to think of me as a kindly eccentric who plants lettuce and radicchio just for them, which is not at all the case. Since the fence has four openings for gates that have yet to be hung, it doesn't effectively deter the rabbits, although it does appear to have discouraged them somewhat. It definitely has not stopped the winter birds, however, which are my arch enemies. They come in increasing numbers each November and stay through March.

One reason the birds are so prolific is the row of shrub roses fifteen feet high and wide that borders the entire length of the potager. The roses, which we think are Duchess d'Orleans, were probably planted in the twenties. An old snapshot of the house taken about that time shows a row of small, shrubby-looking rosebushes dividing the gravel driveway from the fields. When we moved here only one bush remained, about eight feet tall and wide, growing directly across the driveway from the house. It was in full bloom the day my husband and I were married, covered with pale pink blossoms on long arching canes. We became immediately sentimental about the rose, watering and fertilizing it, even though it bloomed only in the month of April.

As we watered, we began to notice minuscule versions of the rose nearby. We watered those and then transplanted them. The driveway is once again lined with magnificent bushes, ideal habitats for the birds who now feed all winter long on my broccoli, lettuces, cauliflower, escarole—in short, on everything but the fava beans, garlic and onion shoots, and the artichoke plants (although they brazenly perch there, surveying where to launch themselves onto the more tender plants).

Since we are not willing to cut down our beautiful hedge of roses, other remedies must be found to the bird problem. I have already tried, with some success, floating row covers—they often floated on the wind despite my weighting them down as instructed—small plastic tunnels (too small), scarecrows, dangling silver spoons, and aluminum foil garlands. I have one more measure to implement, an extreme solution. Next November, just before the birds return from wherever it is they go, I am intent on covering the entire garden in netting. The posts that support the fence are five feet high, and I'm sure that I would happily weed, plant, harvest, and in general maintain my garden unimpeded beneath my ingenious protection. How I will gloat to see the birds stymied and thwarted, my escaroles and frisées pristine and as big as dinner plates, my broccoli and cauliflower with their leaves intact, standing erect, wrapping up the budding heads, no longer pockmarked and shriven. In France, I see whole pear and apple orchards covered with netting, and a nearby asparagus seed farmer covers his entire crop, so surely it will work for my potager.

CREATING A PERSONAL POTAGER

To take the vision of a potager and make it real, you need only a few elements: adequate sunlight and water, well-prepared soil, fertilizer, and a design. Once these are determined, the planting can begin, whether it is spring, summer, or fall.

The first step is to examine the sites you have available that have the requisite three-quarters to a full day of sun. Although some vegetables can be grown with a half day of sun, a potager will suffer in a shady location. Sunlight is important because plants use energy from the sun for growing, and plants lacking adequate sunlight fail to thrive, and, often, to bear fruit. Within the garden itself, plant placement is important because taller or more rapidly growing varieties can shade out others. Taller plants should be strung along a northern border where their shade falls only on the garden edge, or the plant rows should run north and south so the sunlight falls down their length. This is less important in full summer, because the sun is more or less overhead.

Once you have located areas with adequate sunlight, examine the existing or potential water supply. Water should be readily available. A single faucet is enough from which to run a sprinkler or a hose, which is all you need to give your garden the water it needs.

Finally, check your soil. Soil is a mixture of sand, silt, and clay, plus organic matter. Ideally we would all like to have a nice, rich, fast-draining sandy loam that is about one-third each sand, silt, and clay, but that is rarely the case. If your soil is heavy—full of silt or clay—you need to amend it to create pores for air spaces and drainage. This can be done by adding sand, but it is usually more practical to loosen the soil with large amounts of organic amendments like compost, peat moss, or wood fiber. A sandy soil drains too quickly and holds few nutrients, so adding organic amendments also benefits sandy soil. Drainage is important, and if your soil won't drain well, you might consider building raised beds and filling them with a mixture of your soil and organic amendments. This can be a lot of work, but it

solves the soil problem. Planting in containers such as terra-cotta pots is another alternative. In the seasonal chapters, I have given minimum container size for all the vegetables discussed and have indicated any instances where container planting is undesirable. Since drainage is critically important in container planting, the commercial soil mixes should have sufficient organic matter to allow for it.

Plants do best with a soil pH of 6.5 to 7.0, which is a measure of the chemical reaction. Generally, low pH soils are found in rocky stretches or in high-rainfall climates. In arid climates like the American Southwest and much of California, the pH will be high. Inexpensive kits for testing soil pH are available, or you can ask someone locally who is knowledgeable. Soils commonly are improved by adding lime to those with a low pH and gypsum or sulfur to those with a high pH.

When preparing your soil, it is often convenient to add compost or a balanced fertilizer, like a 15-15-15 or a 20-20-20. The numbers indicate, in order, the percentage of nitrogen, phosphorus, and potassium, the main elements needed for plant nutrition. Usually the fertilizer bag carries a guide for the application rate.

Now that you have determined the various areas where you can establish a potager, decide which one suits you best. I loved having a potager in my front yard in town, and it made colorful landscaping. We could have put it in our backyard, but that was a nice fenced area that seemed better left open as a place for our children to play. Consider if you want to be alone when you are in your potager, or whether you would like the company of passers-by and neighbors as you work, and if you want the potager to be a focal point of your landscape or a secondary element.

Size is an important consideration. Remember, since you are only growing vegetables to use on a daily basis, you won't need huge amounts—

in fact, you don't want huge amounts ready for harvest all at the same time. It makes more sense to create small second or third plantings to ensure an ongoing supply.

A small space, perhaps nine feet by twelve feet seems a good beginning. You can always make it larger if you want, and it needn't all be done in a single, work-intensive weekend. A potager is in a constant state of evolvement. The garden of M. Blanc, one of my neighbors in Provence, has become, in my mind, the epitome of a work in progress, while at the same time fulfilling its function of supplying the kitchen.

Over the past seven years, I have watched M. Blanc slowly transform a loose rectangle of rocky, sloping hillside once covered with pubescent oak, scrubby wild juniper, and thistle into a splendid potager. It is the envy, I think, of most of us who live along the road. Before he retired two years ago, M. Blanc was living and working in Marseilles, so he came only on weekends and for the month of August to build his house and work on the garden. After cutting down the trees and digging up the stumps, he dug out all the large rocks. Slowly, his stockpile of rough, grayish white stones grew higher and wider, and the hillside was pitted with craters where they had lain. Next, the scrubby bushes were uprooted, and finally the heavy, dark red clay soil was rototilled. With the rocks dug from the ground, M. Blanc, with various friends and relatives, built a retaining wall along the roadside and another against the steeper slope of the forest to the west, to create a terrace for the garden. The first planting was an olive tree, nearly in the middle.

On my next visit, I noticed that M. Blanc had set out strawberries along the edge of the wall bordering the roadside, and behind them was a long row of artichokes, both perennials of a Provençal potager. At the same time, a toolshed had mushroomed near the rear retaining wall, with a fig tree planted next to it, and in front, an old table, two chairs, plus one old leather armchair. The garden setting is considered highly desirable for a morning *casse-croûte,* or snack, or as a comfortable place to take an afternoon coffee. Gradually his garden, always weed-free, filled up.

In late summer, when M. Blanc's carefully staked tomato plants are loaded with scarlet-red clusters, fall's lettuces are already sprouting beneath, ready to take over when the tomatoes are pulled, and seedlings of cabbages and leeks have already replaced the zucchini. Come winter, the fava beans can be seen pushing their way up in the shelter of the now-huge cabbages and thick leeks. As winter wanes to spring, M. Blanc already has peas emerging as the days lengthen, and again the new lettuces are beneath the artichokes. The shed, in the passing years, has taken on a patina, and looks now as if it has always been there. The plaster over the raw bricks has slowly dappled to ochre and rose and reflects the colors of the land. The olive tree is kept trimmed to about six feet, but the fig, now nearly twelve feet tall, casts summer shade across the little table, and I can see, in the distance, plantings of peach and pear trees. I think I like watching his garden develop over time as much as he has obviously loved creating it.

You can do just as M. Blanc has done: choose any size space and, no matter how weed covered or dismaying it might initially be, establish a prolific kitchen garden. Once the location and size are decided, start to prepare the ground. First clear it of any visible weeds, digging out large rooted ones with a shovel if necessary, and remove as many stones, chunks of cement or brick, or other impediments as possible. Secondly, water the site thoroughly and allow existing weed seeds in the ground to germinate and grow into seedlings, which will take about two weeks. Once the weeds are about one inch high, chop them down with a hoe or turn them into the ground with a shovel or rototiller. Now is the time to add compost or other soil amendments and fertilizer.

The soil must be finely worked to make a clod-free seedbed. That way the seeds, once planted, will be surrounded by small soil particles that will hold moisture close to them during germination and early growth. Loosen the soil as deeply as possible, too. It is important for good drainage, good aeration, and so that the roots can grow freely and not limit the plant's growth.

Now, the fun part: designing your potager. The garden should be personal. It is not only the source of your vegetables, but is also where you spend your time and creative effort in growing the produce for your own kitchen, so it should reflect your tastes and style. What you serve at your table comes from the efforts of your hands and heart, and throughout the seasons brings something special that purchased food cannot.

When I first went to France as a student, long before I had a potager of my own, I marveled, as I still do, at the vegetable gardens that dotted both the rural and urban landscapes. Scraps of land along railroad tracks, irregularly shaped pieces tucked beside rivers, slopes, terraces, front, side, and backyards were all deemed appropriate to fill with vegetables, and no matter the season, the little plots always had something growing. Nearly as intriguing as the kitchen gardens were their accoutrements and their layouts, each an individual work.

Of all the potagers I have ever seen, though, the most stunning was one I came upon years ago on the road to Italy that climbs out of Nice to the northeast, passing through Sospel, below the perched medieval village of Saorge, and above the gorges of the Roya River.

I had taken a narrow side road that turned west out of the village of Fontan and wound up the mountainside, just to see where it would lead. It came to a dead end in a phantasmagoric potager planted on several levels of terraced land on a steep hillside. In the garden were at least five scarecrows dressed in trunkfuls of bourgeois finery of the early 1900s. Empty arms of black serge jackets flapped guard amid teepees of beans and rows of tomatoes. Swirling, once-white petticoats rippled over tightly buttoned hightop boots stuck into stuffed pantalooned legs, forming protection for the young lettuces beneath, while black hats tied with once-black ribbons now greenish bronze with age posed on heads of gourds. Cucumber and bean vines had

wrapped themselves around legs of black broadcloth, climbed across fat, vest-covered torsos, and twisted up beyond cravats and through broken spectacles to hang free in the wind. One scarecrow had a torn lavender silk parasol wired across its shoulders, another a ragged paisley shawl tied around its hips. Pins attached to hats glinted in the sun. Whether or not the birds were scared away from the lush, rich garden of vegetables, I couldn't say, but I was. I backed the car out and away until I could find a place wide enough to turn around, and then headed back to the main road. But I have never forgotten that potager, and I have always thought what fun it must have been to have populated it.

A potager can be quite elaborate in design and decor, like those found at châteaus in the Loire Valley, or it can be utterly plain. To shape a nine-by-twelve-foot space, divide it into twelve squares each roughly three feet on a side. It will be three squares wide at the top and four squares on a side. Plan on running two paths, each about a foot wide, between the squares down the length of the plot. The paths will allow you to reach all parts of the garden without stepping on any plants. If your area is triangular, or otherwise different than a rectangle, simply make your own adjustments, keeping in mind the principle of dividing it into spaces that can be reached by paths.

Once your potager is prepared, what you decide to plant will depend upon the time of year. An understanding of the seasonality of vegetables, that is the stage at which certain vegetables are eaten, is critical. If you are planting in early spring, start with leafy vegetables and quick-growing roots and pods that thrive in cool days, such as lettuces, radishes, carrots, and peas, for a mid- or late-spring harvest. If you are planting in late spring or early summer, when the ground has warmed, you might put in fruiting vegetables, such as beans, squashes, and tomatoes, for summer's first harvest. A potager started in summer might begin with beans, squashes, and tomatoes but also include peppers, eggplants, and pumpkins. Finally, a potager launched in late summer and early fall would need to be planted with short-season, cool-weather vegetables, the same ones that were planted in early spring. But the same garden could also include cabbage, broccoli, and cauliflower seedlings for fall and winter harvest.

The seasonality of vegetables refers to the stage of growth at which a plant is harvested for the table, and different stages of growth generally require different temperatures, growing conditions, and growing seasons. The stages are the vegetative stage, the reproductive stage, and the senescent stage. Another way to express these is preflowering, flowering, and postflowering. Generally the vegetative stage occurs during the cool days of spring or fall, while the reproductive or flowering stage requires longer, warmer days, and the postflowering stage even longer. Thus, tomatoes, which we eat at the fruit stage, require a longer, warmer growing season than do lettuces, which we eat in the leafy stage.

After a seed geminates in the ground, the seedling emerges and vegetative growth begins. The plant issues the array of leaves, stems, and branches that characterizes this stage. Leafy-topped root vegetables such as radishes, carrots, turnips, and fennel are ready for harvest at this stage, as are the lettuces, endives, arugula, basil, cabbages, and radicchio. Some may be harvested within a short thirty days of planting, such as arugula, which can be eaten when the leaves are still immature. Others, like cabbages, require at least sixty days.

Near the end of the vegetative growth, the plant begins to enter its reproductive stage. It puts up stalks followed by buds and flowers. We eat some of our vegetables at the point of budding, such as artichokes, cauliflower, and broccoli.

After the flowers bloom and are pollinated, the plant begins to develop seed for the coming generation, and the plant ovary, which envelopes the seeds, ripens into a fruit. Many vegetables, including tomatoes, cucumbers, squashes, peppers, peas, and beans, are eaten at this stage. Since most plants bloom as the weather warms, if you want a plant for its fruits rather than its leaves, it needs to be put in the earth early enough in spring or summer to allow adequate time for it to pass through the vegetative and flowering stages and to mature.

Once you have designed your garden and decided what to plant, consider planting methods. One technique I use frequently for seeds, especially those of greens, is scatter-planting, which is also known as broadcasting. The seeds are sown in random fashion across the prepared seedbed, then raked in to the appropriate depth. Another method is planting in rows or mounds. I sometimes ignore the suggested planting distances, although not the depth, because those are distances for vegetables grown to standard market size. Instead, I begin picking many of my plants—lettuces, beets, turnips, carrots, leeks, onions, garlic greens—while they are still quite small. Eventually I end up with enough space between the plants to allow for full-size growth.

Seeds should be planted into moist soil. If the ground is dry, water them as soon as possible after sowing. Keep the root zone moist during germination. Small, shallowly planted seeds, such as those for lettuce and basil, will need more frequent watering than larger specimens, like peas and beans, which can be planted more deeply.

Soak transplants in water well before putting them in the ground so that they are fully hydrated and the root ball is moist. This step lessens the effect of transplant shock. Once planted, water again to the depth of the root zone. A few days after planting, apply a dilute mixture of liquid fertilizer.

When planting your potager, keep in mind that the earliest harvest will be from greens planted as soon as the ground can be dug, turned, and raked without clumping. Where I live in northern California that usually means

February. But I have planted peas and lettuces the day after Christmas in years when December was mild and had wonderful crops to harvest in March. My ground warms enough to plant carrots and beets by early April, and it is still a fine time to plant more lettuces, escarole, and frisée for harvest in late May and June, before summer's heat makes them unpalatable, and to plant tomato seeds for summer's harvest.

In May, the ground temperature and the evening air have warmed enough to germinate eggplants, peppers, okra, melons, and beans, which I will harvest throughout summer and into fall. These can be planted in June as well, at the same time as I plant pumpkins, although the harvest will be later.

In late July and August, I plant the broccoli, cauliflower, cabbages, and chicories that will supply my kitchen from fall through spring, as my winter is mild, with temperatures ranging from the midtwenties to the midfifties. In winter here, the whole outdoors acts as a refrigerator for the vegetables, suspending their growth and keeping them crisp and cool.

In September and October, I plant lettuces and other greens for fall and winter harvest, and fava beans to pick in April and May. In December I slip onion and garlic sets into the soil to harvest in early summer.

At my house in California, I have discovered planting times by trial and error. I have planted too early, too late, too much, and not enough. I have waited too long to stake my beans and tomatoes, breaking half of them in the awkward process. I have stood, near to weeping, on a gray, drab day in November, looking at my special Musquée de Provence pumpkins, still dark green, knowing that I had put them in too late and they would never ripen and turn the lovely bronzed buff that I love so much. They have to be planted no later than June 1, and now I know June 20 is too late. I have planted and replanted pole beans in August with no success. The ground was so hot that the water necessary for germination literally boiled the beans in the earth, killing them, which I discovered when I dug down with a knife to see what was wrong.

Only recently have I truly come to believe that the first week or so of February is too early to plant summer squashes. Year after year, the gloriously warm early February days, when the almond trees are blossoming and the sky is a deep cerulean, have tempted me to rush to the potager and get an early start. Many is the Saturday morning I have awakened to a warm, bright day, put off all other plans, rummaged through my seed stash, and spent the day planting. I have never yet had the early summer squashes of my imagination, as the March days are too cold to germinate their seeds. Finally, I have come to accept that on those warm days of false spring, the thing to do is sit in the sun and read or have a picnic. If I am determined to plant, and often I am, I have learned instead to turn to lettuces, peas, and arugula, which like the cool conditions. If the ground isn't too soggy and wet to be worked, they will thrive and bring a crisp harvest to the April kitchen.

As you pursue potager gardening, wherever you live, you will discover when is the right time to plant different vegetables, using the signs of the seasons as they manifest themselves in your particular area. Spring might begin in March or May, but it is still spring and time to plant spring vegetables. Where frost occurs, ask the local extension agent at your state department of agriculture what are the first and last frost dates for your locale. In areas with short growing seasons, seeds of fruiting vegetables may need to be started inside then transplanted to the potager when the ground and weather has warmed sufficiently. In cold-weather climates, mulching may be necessary to protect plants from frost and to prolong the harvest, or season extenders such as plastic tunnels might be incorporated into the potager.

Winter to Spring

At my house the first clue that winter is leaving and spring is arriving is the budding and blooming of the almond trees. Even though the days are often dreary, impenetrable, and gray, the swelling of the buds in late January signals that the earth is getting ready to renew itself.

Sitting in my little office, in the third story of a converted water tower, I can look out across our fields and the country road that runs along them to the banks of the creek that separates us from town. There, the wild almond trees are beginning to show the first of their pinkish white blossoms, long before the nearby elderberry and oak trees leaf out, or the neighboring walnut and apricot orchards show the slightest bit of color. Quickly, in the weeks that follow, bare orchards turn green, daffodils and wild mustard bloom, the air is sweetened by orange blossoms, and spring has arrived.

It is time now to take stock of what is in your potager, what needs to be done in the way of plant removal, cleanup, and ground preparation to get started with spring planting. If you planted broccoli in late summer or early fall for your winter's harvest, you may notice that the buds on the remaining heads are just beginning to open into tiny yellow flowers, soon to be followed by seed. The last of the cauliflower, those you might have planted late, will never come to full size now that the days are lengthening and becoming warmer, and their tiny heads too will soon start to burst into flowers.

Winter is over, and it is time for new growth. In my garden, lifting the heap of brown, scraggly nasturtium vines, which fell to the first frost, I can spot heart-shaped leaves of new seedlings sprouting from the seeds the vines dropped last summer. If your cilantro has weathered the winter, as mine often does, you might find that it has two-foot-high stems, now topped with white flowers. These can be added to a last cabbage salad, for any cabbages remaining in the garden will soon bolt to seed, producing a flower stalk that will burst through the once-solid head. With the warming days, artichokes, which have been standing unchanged since November, suddenly look a little larger, and a hand plunged into the center of the plant reveals soft, pale gray leaves, the first signs of the new growth that precedes the developing flower buds. The favas, if planted in November, are now about one foot high, and growing more each day. By April their pods will be thick and long, full of meaty beans. December-planted garlic and onions haven't grown an inch all winter but now seem to be growing an inch a day. Once they are just a little thicker, they can be pulled and used in the kitchen as green garlic and green onions.

Spring is the most exhilarating of seasons because so many different vegetables can be planted during these two or three months, and growth occurs quickly in the lengthening, warming days. Everything seems possible, which is a great encouragement to clear and prepare the garden quickly and to start planting.

Spring

With the exception of weeds, it causes me pain to dig up anything that is still growing, but once spring has arrived, planting lust takes over, and my imagination is seized by thoughts of new, tender spring vegetables. Perhaps you too will find your winter passion for broccoli, cauliflower, and cabbage spent and decide it is time for them to go to make room for the new season's vegetables. Clearing the potager of the last of winter's plants is like a spring cleaning. When it is over, everything looks pristine instead of cluttered.

The broccoli plants, which now have woody stalks the size of an arm, are not really difficult to remove because their roots are relatively shallow. The same is true of the cauliflower, but the cabbages are different. They have deep tap roots, and once the remaining heads are cut, it is an effort to dig down far enough to remove the thick base. Shriveled nasturtiums and the stark, frost-blackened remains of the basil are easily pulled up and hauled away. All that is left growing in the garden now are the garlic, onions, and favas planted in fall and winter, and the perennial artichokes and strawberries. The remainder of the garden is cleared and empty, ready to till and to plant first with spring's peas, radishes, lettuces, and leafy greens, followed shortly by carrots and beets.

Once the ground is turned, the compost dug in, and the surface smoothed and raked, it is time to start laying out the season's rows and patches. Although four semipermanent paths intersect my garden, the rest is open to reconfiguration throughout the year. So, what were once rows for cabbages now become several smallish rectangles for radishes, arugula, and tat-soi. Former broccoli rows become large rectangles to fill with spinach, lettuces, and chicories. The one-time empty patch becomes a home for beets, and the old nasturtium bed is transformed into a portion of the pea rows.

Peas

Because they can grow to two feet tall or more, peas should be planted in an area that receives three-quarters of a day of sun and where they will not shade out smaller plants. They can act as an attractive backdrop to the rest of the garden as well. The recommended spacing for peas is four inches apart, planted at a depth of one inch. You can plant the seeds much closer, however, thin the young shoots to four inches when just two or three inches high, and use the thinnings in salads, soups, and stir-fries. Once the remaining plants are six to eight inches high, consider providing some support for them, particularly if your area is subject to strong winds that can topple shallow-rooted plants. I prop each plant with a length of pruned branch from a fruit tree. Although manufactured trellises, netting, or stakes and strings can be used as well, I like the aesthetics of the forked dark wood mingled with the twisting tendrils and green of the peas.

Peas require a goodly amount of water while growing, and while in many areas spring rains will supply most of the necessary moisture, in others you will need to be vigilant. Peas need about three-quarters of a day of full sun, but they can tolerate some shade, especially in warm climates, and can be grown in containers at least eighteen inches deep and eighteen inches in diameter.

The first tender pods can be harvested about forty-five days after planting, then shortly thereafter come shelling peas, so sweet and delicate they require just a quick steaming. Many days later, as the peas swell, harden, and their sugar turns to starch, you can cook them down in broth for an hour or so before puréeing it into fresh pea soup.

A number of pea varieties are available, some selected for use as a mature pea, others for their tender edible pods, and still others for best performance in a particular climate. In all instances the pea shoots are edible, as are the first emerging pods. Be sure not to confuse edible pea, also called the English pea *(Pisum sativum)*, with the sweet pea *(Lathyrus odoratus)*, because parts of the latter are poisonous.

Arugula, Tat-soi, and Radishes

All of these short plants can be put nearly anywhere in the garden and will be ready to eat within thirty days after sowing. Rather than arranging them in rows, I like to scatter-plant the seeds into rectangular or square beds in an area that receives at least a half day of sun. I cast them across the surface of the soil, letting them fall where they may, then rake them down about one-half inch deep into the soil. Generally, they space themselves about one-half to an inch apart, with some clusters closer here and there and some more distant. Planting every two weeks assures a steady harvest of tender leaves and young radishes throughout spring, as long as they are kept well watered.

I first observed scatter-planting at Maurice's, where I would periodically spot two-foot squares of earth covered with hundreds of little sprouts of lettuces, spinach, or other vegetables, usually greens. The patch would eventually be thinned, and the thinnings transplanted elsewhere in the garden, or left in place to be plucked and used for salads as soon as they were a few inches tall. It seemed then an immensely practical method, one which I have practiced now for years and highly recommend.

Young arugula leaves only three or four inches long have a mild, slightly nutty flavor. As the plant grows larger, it develops branching stalks, a peppery strong flavor, and coarse, dark green leaves. A wild strain of arugula, with an intense peppery flavor, is available, too. The latter grows initially in a flattish rosette pattern, its stiff, deeply indented leaves widespread and symmetrical, quite different from the loose, flopping leaves of the cultivated variety. As the plant matures, however, it sends forth long, thin, nearly leafless stalks. The flowers of wild arugula are yellow, and those of the cultivated white.

Tat-soi, which is actually an Asian flat cabbage, has a spinachlike flavor and round, rather thick spoon-shaped leaves that form a flat rosette. It grows rewardingly fast, and if you cut the leaves when young rather than letting the plant grow to its full one foot diameter and then harvesting it, a few plants will give you an abundance of tender leaves for salads, stir-fries, and steaming well into late spring.

I have a special affection for radishes because it was through them that I first discovered the power of gardening. My mother gave me a packet of radish seeds and a little trowel and rake, then took me out beneath her bedroom window and showed me where I could dig a small space to plant the seeds. She taught me how to hold the trowel, dig down, turn the soil, and then rake it smooth. After showing me about how deep and how far apart each seed should be planted, she left me to my work. Carefully I poked the seeds, one by one, into the ground and covered them up. One morning,

---

ARUGULA, ORANGE, AND RED ONION SALAD

Peel and section 2 navel oranges. Cut the sections in half crosswise. Combine ¼ cup orange juice, 2 tablespoons red wine vinegar, 3 tablespoons extra-virgin olive oil, and a little salt and pepper to make a dressing. Put the dressing in the bottom of a salad bowl, then add 3 to 4 cups medium-sized arugula leaves, the oranges, and ¼ cup thinly sliced red onion. Pour over the dressing and toss to mix.

only a few days after planting, I opened the window and looked down on my garden to see green sprouts that soon developed into plump red-and-white radishes. I pulled, washed, and served them at dinner every night until they were gone.

Although we typically think of radishes as round and red, there are a number of other varieties, including Easter Egg, a mixture of pink, purple, rose, and white, and the tapering French breakfast types that are red with white tips. These are all short-season types. Larger long-season radishes exist as well, such as the Asian ones, including the long, white daikon type and some with chartreuse exteriors and exquisite rose flesh, and the European black radishes with white flesh. Long-season radishes take nearly twice as long to mature as their short-season relatives do. They are more commonly planted in midsummer for fall harvest. If planted in spring, the lengthening days may cause them to bolt and go to seed.

Radishes, arugula, and tat-soi all need at least three-quarters of a day of full sun, though they can tolerate some shade, and should be kept well watered. In hot weather and dry conditions, the radishes and arugula will become peppery hot, and the tat-soi strong flavored and tough. Radishes and tat-soi for single-leaf cutting can be planted in containers at least twelve inches deep and twelve inches across, while arugula needs vessels at least eight inches deep and eight inches across.

Artichokes

At the opposite end of the spring gardening spectrum from the near-instant gratification of arugula, tat-soi, and radishes are artichokes. When planted from seed, it will be a year to eighteen months before the plants begin to bud. It is a little quicker to grow them from rooted shoots, which if planted in early spring may bud in early summer, although they don't always. Because artichokes are perennials, and in full season grow three to four feet high and as wide, they should be planted in the garden where they will not shade out other plants and will provide a handsome background regardless of season. In my potager, I have two rows that parallel the rear fence. I left enough space between the fence and the last row to plant a row of morning glories to climb the fence and one or two rows of beans, broccoli, or lettuces, depending upon the season.

Most of my artichokes are a variety called Purple Sicilian. The plants, grown from seed five years ago, are wonderfully hardy, unaffected by our frosts, and provide artichokes from late March through early June, unless the weather turns hot early.

Early spring, when the artichokes are just starting to send forth their dusty gray-green inner growth, is the time to separate artichoke divisions. Dig out and remove the new shoots that are growing around the base of each main plant and replant them elsewhere or give them to friends. Maurice, whose family came from Italy, says that he remembers eating these shoots when he was a child. We were talking one February while he was dividing his artichokes, and he gave me a handful of the shoots, their roots trimmed, and told me to try cooking them. Delightedly I went home, washed them, simmered them in salted water, drained them, then added a dressing of olive oil, vinegar, salt, pepper, and minced garlic. I thought they were inedible, but he just laughed when I told him I wasn't able to eat them.

Artichokes need three-quarters of a day of sun, well-drained soil, and adequate water and fertilizer during their growing and budding period in spring and early summer. They can be grown in areas where temperatures do not drop below twenty degrees Fahrenheit for extended periods of time, but elsewhere it is best to protect them with mulch. Since they are perennials, they will need fertilizer available to them before they become vegetative, so provide them with some in midsummer and again in early spring. Once they are through budding in late spring to midsummer, cut back the leaves to within twelve inches of the crowns.

Because artichoke plants are large with deep tap roots traveling up to two feet, they need containers at least three feet deep and three feet in diameter.

Turnips

I am a big fan of turnips and I plant them twice a year, once in early spring and again in late summer or early fall. The tender tops make wonderful additions to stir-fries, soups, and stews, and the tiny new turnips, no larger than a big marble, can be eaten raw or thinly sliced and sautéed in butter for just a few minutes. At the early stage of growth the taste is mild and delicate and the flesh is crystalline.

The more the turnips mature, the stronger and more pronounced the flavor. These need to be cooked longer, and the greens may be too potent to eat at all except for the most devoted lovers of their intense, buttery, mustard-cabbage taste.

A number of turnip varieties are available and some of the most popular are the hybrids first developed by Japanese seed companies in the fifties. Tokyo Cross and Tokyo Market are examples, both creamy white turnips that eventually grow to broad-shouldered roots the size of grapefruits. An exceptional variety popular in the Mediterranean is de Milan, which is small and flattened, with a bright pinkish magenta top.

Turnips grow rapidly. Young, tender roots can often be harvested within thirty days of planting and large, full-grown ones within fifty to sixty days. Plant the seeds only one-quarter inch deep in an area with at least three-quarters of a day of full sun. Give them plenty of water, and then thin the small plants to only five or six inches apart if you plan to harvest them when small or up to a foot apart if you want larger turnips. They can also be planted in containers twelve inches across by twelve inches deep.

Lettuces

Early spring (for me late February and early March), when the weather and ground are still quite cool, is a suitable planting time for lettuces, and six or seven different kinds are not too many. Green and red oakleaf are openheaded cutting types with tender, long, pointed, deeply indented leaves. Bavarian lettuces, the forerunner of iceberg, form loose heads composed of crunchy, ruffled leaves, either green blushed with bronze or ruby. Romaine lettuces have tall, oval heads with crunchy leaves, usually green, although one or two red varieties exist. Each has a distinct flavor.

By mixing the different textures, leaf shapes, colors, and flavors of the lettuces, in combination with greens such as tat-soi, spinach, arugula, and the chicories, you can have a near-endless variety of salads each night for months, even if you use the same vinaigrette. Scatter-plant different lettuces in alternating patches or rows in the garden, to achieve a pattern of colors and textures that is as pleasing to the eye as the tastes are to the palate. Cut

the lettuces leaf by leaf, then leave the heads to grow more leaves, or thin the plants when a few inches tall and use in salads, gradually increasing the space between the plants. A harvesting technique I like to use is to cut the leaves of some, pull others when youngish, and then let the remainder grow to medium or full size.

Plan on at least three-quarters of a day of full sun, cool weather, and plentiful water for your lettuces to grow and thrive. They can, however, tolerate some shade, especially in areas with warm climates. When the weather turns hot, the leaves will toughen and become bitter.

Lettuces that are destined for early harvest can be grown in containers at least eighteen inches in diameter and eight inches deep. If you wish to grow them to full size, deeper, larger containers will be needed.

Green Chicories

The diverse *Cichorium* genus has an extraordinary range of greens and reds that have been most fully exploited in Italy, where an ordinary seed catalog lists a dozen different green chicories and nearly that many red ones; the radicchios, some of which will form tight heads and others which are non-heading; as well as numerous varieties of escarole and endive. When I was in the seed business, I had seeds for over twenty chicories, many of them generous samples from Italian and French seed companies, but these varieties are more difficult to come by now, although a few mail-order companies carry a limited selection. If you are traveling to Italy or France, look for seed packets of interesting-looking chicories or ask traveling friends to do so. The United States Department of Agriculture does not prevent the bringing in of commercially packaged seeds for personal use.

In early spring, plant the green nonheading chicories such as Frastagliata and Puntarelle a Pigna, to harvest in late spring and early summer, and the heading Pain de Sucre. The young thinnings of all of them make delightfully bitter additions to salads. The mature plant of Frastagliata yields thick, white succulent midribs bulbed at the base, their uppermost edges lined on either side with sawtoothed green leaves that can be chopped and

Italian Chicories
and Roasted Wood Duck

Rub 2 wood ducks, each about 1 pound, with salt and pepper, then with a nubbin of butter. (Or use 1 Muscovy or other duck.) Fill the cavities to overflowing with fresh thyme. Place in a baking dish just large enough to hold them, along with ½ cup dry white wine. Roast at 450 degrees F for about 45 minutes, or until the juices run clear with only a hint of pink when pierced with a knife tip. Keep the ducks warm while you prepare the greens.

Add ½ cup dry white wine to the roasting pan and bring to a simmer, scraping up any clinging bits and reducing to about ½ cup. Measure 4 cups mixed very young Frastagliata and Puntarelle a Pigna chicories, escarole, arugula, and spinach leaves. Arrange the greens on 4 plates and pour the warm reduced juices over them. Cut the ducks in half with kitchen shears and place one half on each plate.

then cooked with garlic and olive oil, Roman style. Puntarelle a Pigna forms distinct stalks of pale green that are twisted and whorled and can be cooked in the same manner. Pain de Sucre develops into a tight, full, elongated head up to eighteen inches tall, with blanched, ivory-green inner leaves wrapped around one another in an upward spiral. It is one of the milder chicories, resembling somewhat the inner leaves of escarole. Another favorite is San Pasquale chicory, which greatly resembles dandelion and is often sold in markets as such.

The seeds may be sown like lettuce seeds, which they resemble, scatter-planted, or planted in rows. The green chicories all require at least three-quarters of a day of full sun, and while they are difficult to overwater, they are more tolerant of dry conditions than lettuces are.

Chicories have deeper tap roots than do lettuces and require containers at least twelve inches deep and eighteen inches in diameter, although if you want to grow them to full size, you will need an even larger and deeper container.

Escarole and Frisée

From the chicory genus also comes frisée, which is a fine-leaved endive, and escarole. As with the lettuces, a number of different varieties exist from which you can choose, including the less familiar frisées such as Fine Maraîchère and Fine de Louvier and the tall, heading Cornet de Bordeaux escarole.

Escarole and frisée can be sown in early spring and, like the green chicories and lettuces, can be scatter-planted or planted in rows. Since their leaves are rather coarse and bitter when green, they are usually preferred blanched. Blanching is the process in which a growing plant is deprived of sunlight to reduce its production of green chlorophyll. Thus, the blanched leaves of escarole and frisée, typically the center leaves, are not green but pale ivory, tender, and mild. Yet they still have the underlying hint of bitterness that makes them so desirable.

The heads of escarole and frisée one sees in France are enormous, often eighteen inches in diameter, with blanched centers easily spanning twelve inches. Blanching can be accomplished in a number of ways. I once visited a production farm near Lyon that grew escarole and frisée for salad-mix factories, and there I saw acres and acres of escarole and frisée plants covered with white plastic half domes twelve inches in diameter. One dome was placed on every plant to blanch the growing centers. Terra-cotta pots, with the bottom hole sealed, can be placed over the centers of the growing plants to block the light, or the plants can be caught up with a rubber band when they are about ten inches in diameter and the bands left for ten days to two weeks, but no longer. In general, whatever blanching method you choose, start when the innermost leaves of the plants have begun to grow tightly together and the plants themselves are nearly full size.

The easiest method, which causes the plants to self-blanch and the one that I most frequently use, is to scatter-plant the escarole and frisée, then thin the plants to three or four inches apart. As the plants get larger, the outer leaves are pushed up and around each head by the neighboring plants, thus creating a self-blanching environment. When the centers are nicely blanched, I cut out the hearts with a knife, taking only the blanched leaves. Replacement leaves will grow until the weather becomes too hot. Both escarole and frisée are best watered at their bases, rather than by overhead sprinkling. Otherwise, as they mature, they can develop rot in the tightly packed hearts, especially during blanching.

Escarole and frisée require at least three-quarters of a day of full sun, although in areas with warm climates they can tolerate some shade. They can be planted in containers, but their deep tap roots and large size require a large container, at least two feet deep and two feet across.

Strawberries

Strawberries, if a potager contains them (and not all do), have a certain pride of place because they are the early garden fruit of spring and summer, appearing well before the melons ripen. Like artichokes, strawberries are perennials and should be planted where they will have enough space for the runners, which can reach two feet long, and where they will be aesthetically pleasing in the garden. In many French potagers, they are planted in two rows along one of the garden edges. That way they don't interfere with the comings and goings of the annual plantings that comprise most of the garden and also provide a pretty border.

It can be a painstaking task to grow strawberries from seed, so transplants, which are easily and quickly started, are recommended. Plant them about twelve inches apart. Most varieties, of which there are many, will produce fruit within forty-five days, some only in summer, others from spring through summer.

Keep strawberries well watered. Fertilize them when planted, and then several times throughout the year and again in the spring when the first new green shoots appear. In mild-winter climates, strawberries need no special treatment, but elsewhere they should be heavily mulched or otherwise protected from frost.

Strawberries can be grown successfully in containers that are at least twelve inches across and eighteen inches deep. There are even special containers called strawberry pots or jars, usually about two feet tall, that have pockets for planting strawberries.

Carrots, Spinach, and Beets

When the ground has warmed a bit, in early to mid-April for me, carrots, spinach, and beets can be planted. Carrots are a bit tricky to grow, because their deep roots can be deformed by heavy clay soil. Sandy loam is preferable, but should you have a heavy soil, choose a round carrot variety such as Planet.

SAUTÉED CARROTS
WITH CHERVIL

Melt a nubbin of butter in a skillet and add about 3 cups thinly sliced mature carrots. Sprinkle with a little salt and pepper and sauté until the edges are nearly golden. Stir in 1 tablespoon minced fresh chervil. Serve hot.

Until recently, I haven't had much success with carrots. I don't know whether it was because I lost patience with their slow growth (I always think they should grow at the same pace as the radishes, but they don't), because I hadn't prepared the ground well, or simply because I didn't eat or cook with them often. In any case, I gave them short shrift in my potager. But now, I have had a happy success with a French variety called Touchon, which is a tapering, semilong type. I plant the seeds close together in rows, then begin to dig the young carrots once I can see they are about one-quarter inch wide at the neck where the leaves meet the root. These are delicate, sweet, pale orange roots, perfectly straight and four to six

inches long, a fine component in spring vegetable stews. I continue to dig the remaining carrots as I need them, and when they are fully mature, about sixty days after planting, they are ten inches long, an inch in diameter, and have turned to a deep, meaty red orange. Throughout summer, through even the hottest weather of July and August, they retain their sweet, juicy flavor and handsome color. Not until fall, when they have begun to flower, do I finally dig up the few survivors and take them to the compost pile. Long carrots can be grown in containers at least two feet deep and eighteen inches across. Round varieties will flourish in containers only one foot deep and one foot across.

Spinach has become a very important member of my spring potager. As a child I detested creamed spinach, ranking it, along with stewed tomatoes, at the bottom of my vegetable list. Then one night, many years later, I discovered how misguided I had been. Mme Corbet, who lives across the road, had invited my husband and me over for dinner and served a first course of a lovely cold rabbit terrine she had made, accompanied with tiny cornichons. The second course took me aback. It was a large, shallow baking dish filled with creamed spinach and set with about a dozen hard-boiled eggs, halved. It was delicious. She explained that it was the final harvest of spinach from her potager, a yield of four large bushel baskets, that I had seen earlier in the day near the outdoor sink, waiting to be washed. Although I don't think she used all of it, I bet she used nearly half, because I have discovered a goodly amount of fresh spinach is required to make a decent portion of creamed spinach, or *épinards au gratin*.

ÉPINARDS AU GRATIN

Blanch plenty of spinach in boiling water until just limp. Drain and rinse with cold water. Squeeze dry and chop. Set aside while you make a béchamel sauce. When the sauce is done, put a nubbin of butter in a skillet and sauté some minced shallots for a few minutes, then add the spinach and sauté for a minute or two. Add enough sauce to the spinach to bind it. Put in a gratin dish and bake at 350 degrees F for about 20 minutes, or until piping hot.

Combine 2 ounces Gorgonzola cheese with about ¼ cup extra-virgin olive oil, 2 tablespoons red wine vinegar, and a little pepper, mashing the cheese with a fork until all is well mixed. Pour the dressing into the bottom of a salad bowl, then add 4 cups young spinach leaves. Turn to coat the leaves. Add ¼ cup coarsely chopped toasted walnuts and turn them in, along with 1 ounce crumbled Gorgonzola. Garnish with several more tablespoons of toasted walnuts.

Now I allocate an area of at least four feet by six feet for spinach alone. This I plant in rows, the seeds about two inches apart in rows about six inches apart. I am generous with the space because although I certainly harvest some of the young leaves for salads and quick sautés, I am mostly interested in a plentiful harvest of the large, fully mature leaves for cooking. Spinach is a heavy user of nitrogen, so I fertilize the plants when they have six leaves, and again if they show any signs of yellowing. Although a number of spinach varieties are available, my favorite is Melody, a hybrid with smooth, substantial leaves and a fine flavor.

Spinach requires at least half a day of sun and should be kept well watered. It can be grown in containers at least eighteen inches across and eighteen inches deep.

I plant only a short row of beets. It's not because I don't like them, but rather because they grow slowly—it takes about forty-five days from seed until the roots are an inch in diameter—and by the time they are ready to harvest, I want their ground for summer squashes or cucumbers.

Some years I simply plant beets for their greens, which are wonderful in salads or braised like spinach, and then turn the rows over to plantings for summer. When planting for roots, sow the seeds about three inches apart and one-half inch deep in rows eight inches apart. Whether planting for tops or roots, keep the beets well watered.

Beets can also be planted in containers twelve inches across by eighteen inches deep.

Spring to Summer

As spring days become warmer and longer, I am lost in the seasonal pleasures of picking fava beans, pulling onions and radishes, and cutting artichokes and lettuces for the kitchen, but it is time to start planting summer vegetables. At every meal, spring's bounty is in evidence. At aperitif time, crispy radishes and baby favas appear along with salt for dipping and baguette slices spread with butter. Homemade pizzas topped with artichokes and bits of grilled green garlic and onions and ragout of lamb with young, tender peas and carrots are frequent main dishes, while an endless variety of mixed lettuces and greens are the accompaniments.

Yet, even in the midst of this lush harvest, the potager gardener has to think about planting for the summer harvest. The cyclical nature of potager gardening is a joy, as the anticipation that comes with planting for future meals is always occurring at the same time as the instant gratification of the daily harvest.

Even as the lettuces are in their full glory, I know that soon the imminent onset of summer's heat will make them bitter and their place at the table will be usurped by sweet tomatoes. So, in the interest of the coming months, I start pulling out *some* of the lettuces in midspring and convert their space to a bed for tomato seeds.

By late spring, the radishes, although still crunchy, are becoming large and peppery, and soon to become pithy. These are pulled, too, and their space planted to basil or dill.

As the last of the fava beans are harvested, now meaty and full of starch, perfect for purées and soups, their ground is cleared and turned, then planted with beans or okra. The winter-planted garlic and onions have now bulbed, and their tops are dried and drooping. It is time to pull them and lay them out to cure, and to ready their space for hills of summer squashes and cucumbers.

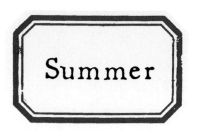

Summer

SUMMER'S ARRIVAL AND SPRING'S DEPARTURE ARE ABRUPT IN NORTHERN California. The cool spring days with their morning mist and evening chill rapidly give way to bright, hot mornings and warm nights. The rolling oak-dotted hills that are so distinctive to the local landscape turn quickly from lush green to their summer color of bright straw yellow, with no more green grass to be seen until the rains of October bring a brief flush before winter sets in. The bloom in the orchards is long gone, and the leafy trees are hiding their swelling fruits.

In the garden, it is time to pull out the early plantings of spring greens and peas, to dig the last of the radishes, and to make way for the first of the summer plantings. I love the idea that even as I gather frisée, escarole, lettuce, and baby leeks for dinner, I am looking forward to the harvest of the newly planted tomatoes, eggplants, cucumbers, corn, melon, and okra.

Pulling out the spring garden is not nearly as difficult as clearing away the remains of the winter garden. Most of the radishes and turnips have already made their way to the table, and their space is nearly empty. The roots of the peas, arugula, tat-soi, and other greens, planted only eight or ten weeks earlier, offer little resistance when you hand-pull them, and even the onions and garlic, planted in winter, can be easily dug, ready as they are to come from the earth now that their bulbs are swollen and full. Once the spring vegetables are removed, the ground can be turned and worked, then raked smooth again for planting.

In my garden, I leave the spring-planted lettuces, escarole, frisée, and spinach as long as I can because they are such basics of my kitchen. I dig and turn them over only when they have become too bitter from the heat to be tasty, but in a milder summer climate than mine they could be left in the ground even longer. The beets and carrots, still small, are already being pulled a few at a time, and soon their space will be empty. Chicories, too, are in the process of being harvested. The artichokes and strawberries are perennials so they, of course, will stay in place. My family enjoys strawberries throughout the summer, but by early June it is already too hot for the artichokes, so I cut these back and remove all the large leaves and stems, leaving only a few buds to bloom with their inimitable blue-purple blossoms.

Summer planting is unusual because vegetables for both summer and fall and even winter harvest are being planted, so it is the busiest, most jam-packed time of the year in the potager. It is also one of the most difficult because you must gather the mental strength in late summer to start replacing eggplants, cucumbers, corn, and beans with the broccoli, cauliflower, and kale that will eventually provender the fall and winter tables.

In laying out the new plantings in early summer, give special thought to placement in the garden in relationship to water. Unlike spring-planted vegetables, which can be given approximately the same amount of water, summer plantings have varying moisture needs. Corn is a heavy user of water and beans only slightly less so, but excessive watering of tomatoes causes them to be increasingly vegetative rather than to flower and produce fruit, and later, once the fruits have ripened, too much water can cause splitting. Melons and pumpkins need a lot of water during their early stages of growth and for the fruits to fill, but during the last ripening days should have little or no water for they, too, risk bursting. Peppers, both sweet and hot, and eggplants have about equal water needs. Where you live will determine how much your water needs are served by Mother Nature's summer rains rather than the garden hose. But keep in mind that seasonal droughts are not unheard of in areas that boast August showers.

Tomatoes

Even though they are, in fact, fruits, tomatoes are ranked as America's number-one favorite vegetable. For me, the first bite of a true sun-ripened tomato picked from the vine is the hallmark of summer, and in my enthusiasm, I sometimes overplant them, cheating on the spacing rule of one foot apart in rows three feet apart, and instead plant them in rows two feet apart, always in full sun. When I set out the three-inch-high seedlings, I find it hard to believe that each one will grow and spread to become at least four feet tall and two feet wide, even when contained by stakes and strings.

GREEN TOMATO
AND CILANTRO SALSA

Chop green (unripened) tomatoes. Mix with chopped cilantro, red onion, a little garlic, salt, pepper, and lime juice. Add minced fresh chilies for a spicier salsa, avocado for a spreadable one.

Tomatoes can be planted into cold ground if frost is not an issue. My neighboring farmers in northern California often begin sowing in January when the temperatures are in the high thirties.

If you decide to grow them from seed (and if you want the more unusual varieties, heirlooms such as

Brandywine or Marvel Stripe, you will need to, as these are rarely available as transplants), you can plant every three or four inches, then thin to the desired spacing. It's difficult at the beginning because the garden looks so bare, and it is hard to believe that the tiny seedlings will be huge vines in a few short months. It isn't catastrophic, however, if the vines begin to close off the paths between the rows or otherwise take over more than their own space, as they can be pruned both on the top and sides. Cut off the offending pieces of vine just above a leaf. More will grow to take their place.

Tomatoes are either bush types, which grow to about two feet tall, or vine types, either determinate or indeterminate. Determinate types will grow to a specific height, perhaps four or five feet, and indeterminate vines will simply keep on growing with no predetermined height. If you are growing tomatoes in a small space, consider bush and determinate types, or plan on pruning.

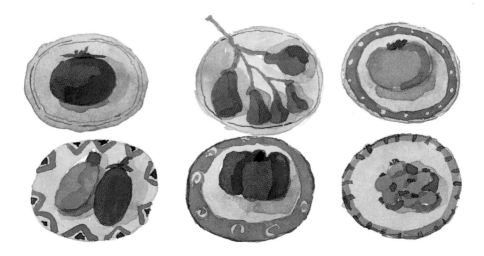

Two of the great changes in American vegetable gardening in the last ten years are the commercial resurrection of heirloom tomato seeds and the development of new and interesting varieties for the home and market gardener, not just the large-scale grower. Today, not only can we buy these tomatoes at farmers' markets all over the country, but we can purchase the seeds from a number of different sources. My personal favorites of the cherry-tomato types are the ultrasweet, marble-sized Sungold, the almost equally sweet Sweet 100s, and the Green Grape, with its balanced flavor and its bright chartreuse flesh. Of the medium size, I like the golden-striped Green Zebra, also with chartreuse flesh, the delicately flavored White Wonder, and the Black Prince, with its dark green shoulders and deep purplish flesh. The tart, acidic taste of the Italian heirloom, Costoluto Genovese, forces me to rate it my favorite among the large tomatoes, with Brandywine and Marvel Stripe close seconds.

Different tomato varieties require varying numbers of days to ripen, anywhere from forty-two days for Early Girl to eighty plus for some Italian types like Costoluto Genovese. If you have a short growing season, it is best to choose varieties that mature early, rather than the late-maturing types. If you live in an area with a long, warm summer, consider the long-maturing varieties, typically the large Beefsteak. A mixture of early, midseason, and late is ideal, as you will have new tomato varieties ripening throughout the season, adding extra excitement in the kitchen. I follow my neighbor Françoise's style from July through mid-October, eating tomatoes every day—usually twice a day. I make fresh tomato sauce for pasta, tomato-and-basil salad, fresh tomato stews, broiled tomatoes, tomato-and-bread salad, and we never get tired of them.

Bush tomatoes can be grown in containers at least eighteen inches in diameter and eighteen inches deep. Vining types are not suitable for container growing.

Sweet Peppers and Chilies

Pepper seeds require warm, moist soil to germinate and may take as long as eight or nine days before the first seedlings appear. Because of the careful attendance needed in the garden until germination and early growth, I find that peppers are good candidates for transplanting rather than seeding directly into the garden. If you have the space, you might start your own seeds in flats and, once they have six leaves, transplant them to the garden. Numerous varieties of sweet peppers—especially those favored in Italy and France, such as the sweet Bull's Horn, Corno di Toro, and the super-sweet, blocky Quadrati d'Asti bells—are not available as transplants and you will need to grow these treasures from seed. The same is true for many chilies, unless you live in the southwest. Mulato, a rich, green-brown pepper with an earthy bite, poblano, the classic black-green stuffing pepper, and strains of bird's eye chilies are among those that I have never found as transplants, and these I grow from seeds.

Nurseries tend to carry transplants of the more familiar serrano, jalapeño, and Anaheim chilies, and sweet peppers including purple, gold, red, and white bell peppers as well as 'Gypsy' and pimiento. 'Gypsy' is a favorite in my garden, because, while it is neither thick-meated nor as sweet as the bell-peppers, it arrives in the kitchen sooner. It first colors a light chartreuse to pale yellow, and as it matures, turns to orange, much as a green bell pepper goes from green to red. If you have a long growing season, about seventy-five growing days once you have set out the transplants, you can grow the very thick-walled, super-sweet heart-shaped pimiento. Most chilies require the same number of growing days to mature, with the serranos and jalapeños taking a bit less. Remember, peppers may be harvested at the green stage, but they grow sweeter with time, changing color as they mature.

Space pepper plants, sweet or hot, about twelve inches apart. If you are sowing seeds, space them four inches apart, then thin to twelve inches. Peppers are quite suitable for container growing and make beautiful decorative plants. The containers should be at least eighteen inches deep and twelve inches in diameter.

ROASTED RED PEPPER, GOAT CHEESE, AND TAPENADE SANDWICHES

Spread 1 slice of toasted bread with fresh goat cheese and another with tapenade. Put a layer of roasted red peppers and one of fresh basil leaves between them to make a sandwich.

Eggplants

Warm soil and at least three-quarters of a day of full sun are needed for egg-plants to germinate. Maurice gauges their planting time by the oak trees. When the trees' first new green leaves appear sometime in May, he knows the ground is warm enough to sow the eggplant seeds, and then he keeps the ground moist, but not saturated, until the seedlings emerge, about seven days later.

Eggplants grow to about two feet tall and about twelve inches in diameter and are best planted where they will not shade out other plants. Their leaves can be used to shade lettuce seedlings from the hot sun in later summer, however.

If you are growing from seed, space the seeds two to three inches apart and then thin to a foot apart, the same distance at which seedlings are planted. Since a number of excellent eggplant varieties are available as transplants at nurseries in late spring and summer, you might want to purchase seedlings rather than plant seeds. Two long Japanese types, Millionaire and Ichiban, have glossy, deep purple skin and calyxes and rapidly produce harvest-size fruits about forty-five days after transplanting. Black Beauty is the traditional globe eggplant, and I can find no fault with its flavor or appearance. It takes about sixty days to produce harvest-size fruits. Unfortunately, one of the loveliest of all eggplants, the Italian Rosa Bianco, is rarely available as seedlings at nurseries. Instead, you will have to sow the seed of this lavender-and-white-striped globular beauty with delicate pure white flesh, but it is worth the extra trouble.

Eggplants can be grown in containers at least eighteen inches in diameter and two feet deep.

Cucumbers

Although cucumbers are a traditional part of the summer potager, you need only two or three plants to keep you supplied with a harvest for slicing throughout the season. A number of varieties are available, and it is educational to change varieties from year to year. The Armenian cucumber is ridged and has pale green, smooth skin. When it is small, eight to ten inches long and tender, it needs no peeling. Its slices are beautiful scalloped rounds. The flavor is sweet and the texture crunchy. Another unusual type is the Lemon cucumber, which is about the size of a small apple and is a light, creamy yellow when ready to eat.

Quick to grow from seed, cucumbers are traditionally planted in mounds in the garden, surrounded by a moat. Shape each mound about two feet in diameter, and make three holes one-half inch deep in the mound. Plant six seeds, two to each hole. Eventually thin the plants to the three strongest. Fill the moat with water to saturate the root zone slowly. Once blooms appear along the vines, the cucumbers follow shortly. If you like them small, keep them well surveilled, because like zucchini, they quickly go from petite to gigantic. They can also be planted in rows, farm style.

Cucumbers can be planted in containers that are at least eighteen inches in diameter and two feet deep. The vines can sprawl across the ground, or some support, such as a trellis, can be provided.

Cucumber Salad

Thinly slice peeled or unpeeled cucumbers and mince red onions. Combine these in a bowl with dill, cilantro, basil, tarragon, or a mixture. Sprinkle with salt and pepper and add rice wine vinegar. Mix well and refrigerate for at least an hour before serving.

Corn and Okra

I can't imagine an American harvest garden without sweet corn. But if your potager space is small, you may have to forgo this backyard classic. Corn is pollinated by the wind moving pollen from the male tassels on top to the receptive silks on the female ear. The rows should run up and down the prevailing wind. In a large field of corn, ample pollen moves around on the air, but in a small, thin planting all the silks may not be struck. The poor fertilization results in ripe ears with many missing kernels. If you have the space, sow seed one and one-half inches deep and six inches apart, setting rows twelve to eighteen inches apart

In my first California potager I felt I had space only for two rows. They were five feet long and I planted them with some exotic seeds called Blue Tortilla. I wanted to dry the kernels and then grind them to make blue tortillas, which I had read about in a magazine review of a southern California restaurant. The corn grew to well over six feet, sported long tassels, and eventually I saw some ears forming, swelling within their husks, but not many. Some stalks had none at all, others one or two. I had to try the corn fresh because the kernels were a beautiful pale lavender. I picked two of my ten ears, cut the kernels from the cob, and mixed them with the kernels of some white corn I had purchased at a farm stand. The result was delicious. The lavender kernels were very starchy and cornlike, while the sweet corn was very sugary, with little starch taste. The remaining ears I allowed

CREAMED FRESH CORN

Cut the kernels off several ears of corn into a bowl, being sure to capture the milk from the kernels as well. Heat a nubbin of butter in a saucepan, then add the corn, salt, and pepper and sauté for a minute or two. Add just enough cream to cover, and cook until somewhat thickened. Add chopped fresh cilantro and serve.

to dry down and then I picked. The kernels were a dark slate-gray–blue, but some of the ears were malformed. I did save them but never ground them into meal.

Six okra plants supply my kitchen with plenty of pods for frying, pickling, and making gumbos and soups. The seeds, planted eight to ten inches apart when the ground is thoroughly warm (in late May and June for me), grow quickly, and the plants soon reach two feet tall. At that point they begin to bloom with beautiful soft yellow blossoms that resemble hibiscuses, followed shortly by the pointed, ridged pods. I pick the pods when quite small, only two or three inches long, because they are so tender then and cook quickly. The larger pods, with their mature seeds, require a longer time on the stove. The mucilaginous quality of okra, which puts off some people, dissipates during cooking.

Container planting is not suitable for corn or okra.

Green Beans and Shelling Beans

Growing green beans in your potager offers the opportunity to be inventive about supports for them to twist and climb, a good reason to plant such vining varieties, sometimes called pole beans, as the thin, meaty French haricot vert. Emerite, developed by the French seed company Vilmorin and available in the United States by mail order, is my current favorite of the vining types. Bamboo poles or fruit-tree prunings tied into teepee shapes are common in the French countryside, while a chicken-wire fence or chicken-wire cages are more typically found in the United States. Sometimes I plant the pole beans in combination with morning glories on teepee supports. This makes quite a spectacular sight, as the blue and scarlet morning glories twist up the poles along with the deep green leaves of the vines, all of them, as summer progresses, lengthening and waving their tendrils and blossoms out away from the teepees and creating their own forms. In areas with mild summer climates, vining nasturtiums can be planted on the teepees as well.

You can construct circular teepees using long bamboo lengths or branches stripped of leaves. Push them into soft ground at an angle, allowing the tops to cross about one foot down from their upper ends. Tie them together with heavy twine at the crossing point. Plant the seeds around the base of the teepee about three inches apart. It is important that the poles be well sunk, because the fully planted structure becomes a sail in the wind and can be blown over. I have gone out to my potager more than once to see its skyline changed and toppled teepees on the ground.

Not all green beans are vining types, though. In fact, most of the newer varieties seem to be bush beans, which grow a foot or a foot and a half high. They too should be planted about three inches apart. There are literally dozens of varieties, old, new, and heirloom, and while I vary somewhat, I find that a fine-fleshed yellow wax bean such as Roc d'Or, developed from the French heirloom Beurre de Roquencourt, and one or two flat Italian beans serve my kitchen needs

Shelling beans also have a place in the potager. Green beans, whether bush or pole, are eaten when immature, with lots of pod "meat" but before the seeds are fully developed. As the seeds grow, the pods become fibrous. Shelling beans, on the contrary, are savored not for their pod, but for the beans inside. Lima beans, black-eyed peas, kidney beans, cranberry beans, and flageolet beans are all shelling types. The beans come in a wide range of colors and flavors, but if I have room for only one, I grow Italian borlotto beans, either the bush or vining type, which are similar to our cranberry beans but meatier and larger. As the pods develop, they turn a brilliant scarlet and cream, which is repeated in the seeds inside. Fresh shelling beans are reason alone to tend a potager, as they are not easy to find in markets, even farmers' markets, and are a true seasonal specialty: once the beans are fully formed and mature, it is a short passage from toothsomely tender to the tooth-breaking hard, dry bean.

Late summer through early fall is the time for fresh shelling beans, depending upon when they were planted and the variety. Once the plants have begun to shut down, and the pods begin to dry and the beans harden, I like to harvest some of the plants and dry the beans to use during winter. This is easily done. Leave the pods on the plant until they are paper-dry and just beginning to crack open, then pick them into a large paper bag or a box. Next, separate the beans from the dried pods by rubbing the pods between your hands until they shatter and fall away, freeing the dried beans. The remaining "trash" can be removed by blowing or by tossing the beans in the wind. Discard the smaller or shriveled beans, then store your clean dried beans in an airtight tin or plastic container. They should be used within the year, as older beans take longer to cook. Besides, a new harvest will be in.

To showcase the distinct flavors of individual shelling beans, cook them on their own with a little winter savory and eat them hot, or let them cool for use in a summertime salad. They can also be combined with garlic, tomatoes, and squashes to make soups. Besides borlotto beans, other shelling bean favorites of mine are flageolets, cannellini, and limas.

Regardless of type or variety, bean seeds are subject to rotting if planted too early into soil still cold and soggy. They need at least three-quarters of a day of full sun and a goodly amount of water. Ideally in areas with hot summers, beans are planted in very late spring, early summer, and late summer, and in areas with a mild summer climate, in early to midsummer. If one week after planting, no seedlings have broken through the soil, dig down to the planting depth, which should be one to one and one-half inches, and see what has happened to the seeds. If they have indeed rotted, plant again.

Bush and vining beans can be grown in containers at least eighteen inches in diameter and eighteen inches deep. The vining beans can be left to sprawl across the ground or they may be provided with a support.

Melons

Maurice taught me to revere melons. He loves to eat them as well as to grow them and he is never as happy as when he has a perfect melon to pass around the table so everyone can exclaim over its intense flavor. He never says much himself, just smiles and takes another slice or goes and gets another melon. Bringing the melon to the table is Maurice's domain, and just before time to serve it, he arises to go down to the *cave* where he keeps those he picked that day for the house.

He prepares them for their destiny—sweet, ripe, succulent—by nursing them from the time they are seedlings, visiting them at least twice a day, making sure they are thriving. He plants them in late April and early May, and, if the weather turns cold and rainy in May, as it can in Haute Provence, and he loses the first plantings, he sows again in late May, even into mid-June. Although he plants a goodly amount of Charentais melons for the hordes of *estivans,* the summer visitors who flock to the region in August, he also plants Jaune Canary and Les Américains, a winter keeper melon that he sells in September and October. The seeds for these two he saves from year to year, but he buys fresh hybrid Charentais seed new each year. For twenty

years he has been known in the region as having the best melons in the markets of Riez and Aups, and the same customers have been coming to him season after season, tourists and locals alike, bypassing other vendors to wait instead in his line for melons. He and Françoise can tell customers which melons are ready for lunch that day, which ones are for dinner, and which for dinner and lunch the next day. These are melons harvested with a keen eye and a passion for the fruit itself. In melon season Maurice alone must eat at least six melons a day—one at breakfast, one at lunch, one for dinner, and the others consumed as samples in the field.

In my own garden, I learned why he visits his melons several times a day. A melon that is not ripe in the morning can slip from the vine into my hand by late afternoon or early evening. Left until the next morning, it will have ripened yet another degree, perhaps to a dinnertime melon. Unpicked until the following morning, it will be so ripe that it must be eaten at lunch.

Because melons, like pumpkins, require a lot of space in the garden, it can be difficult to fit them into a potager. When space is limited, consider planting your melons near tall plants that have open spaces between the ground and their leaves, such as eggplants or artichokes, so the vines can spread out beneath them. As long as melons receive the water they need without overwatering the nearby plants, this is a good solution.

Melons, like cucumbers and summer squashes, can be planted in two-foot-diameter mounds, surrounded by a moat. Plant the seeds about one inch deep, three or four together, in three or four equidistant places on the mound. Thin to the strongest plant per group when the seedlings have four to six leaves. Melons can also be planted in patches or rows.

I plant Charentais melons because, in my opinion, a perfectly ripe Charentais is one of the most delectable of seasonal delicacies, and they remind me of happy summers in France. Charentais melons are true cantaloupes, unlike the popular American cantaloupe, which is really a muskmelon. As many melons ripen, they develop an abscission layer where the stem meets the fruit, so that when the fruit is mature it "slips" away from the stem. This is the case with American cantaloupes: it is easy to see the circular crack growing and widening around the end of the stem and, when quite ripe, the melon can be picked up in your hand and rolled back off the stem. It doesn't come readily if it is not ripe. Charentais melons, however, don't slip, so you must watch the straw color move into the skin and, especially, watch the two leaves on the vine that are closest to the stem. As the melon ripens, those two leaves will begin to die, their impending demise apparent because of the yellow mottling that appears, shortly followed by browning. With diligent practice, by watching the stages of those leaves, you can choose your stage of ripeness.

There must be enough water in the soil for the melons to fill and develop their size, but avoid watering heavily during the final stages of ripening. Too much water can cause splitting and dilute the sugars.

Melons, like pumpkins, are not suited for container growing.

Basil, Dill, and Cilantro

The green herbs, basil, dill, and cilantro, are the seasoning backbone of the potager from June through October. Although you can plant these in late spring, they can also be planted in small successive plantings from early to midsummer to ensure an ongoing supply of tender leaves.

If I am in Provence in early summer, even if only for a few weeks, I buy three or four basil plants at the open market. They come wrapped in newspaper and tied with twine. I disrobe them, pot them, and keep them on my windowsill. Maurice also has several kinds of basil in the potager, including some purple basil grown from seeds I gave him. He is even growing cilantro now that Françoise has ventured into Chinese and Thai cookery, using recipes supplied by Mme Corbet, who is quite an adventuresome cook.

A dozen or more varieties of basil are available, including lemon basil and cinnamon basil, but by far the most common is the large-leaved Italian basil. Nurseries usually have a plentiful supply of seedlings in late spring and early summer, but basil is also easy to grow from seed. Scatter-planting basil seeds and then raking them in to a depth of about one-half inch is effective, or they can be planted in rows and thinned to four inches apart.

Dill and cilantro are easy and quick to grow from seeds, and these water-loving herbs, like basil, can be scatter-planted and then raked in to a depth of one-half inch to make lush cutting patches. The cilantro and dill are both quick to flower and go to seed, so successive plantings from early to mid-summer ensure a steady supply of fresh leaves.

Basil, dill, and cilantro can be planted in containers at least twelve inches deep and eight inches across.

Summer Squashes

Like radishes, summer squashes are always good to plant because they are sure to be quick evidence of success. In that first front-yard potager, the zucchini ripened ahead of everything else. We were enormously pleased with ourselves as every day we cut squashes from the plants and shared them with our neighbors. Our children trundled up and down the street with their little wagon full of the squashes, letting the neighbors choose what they wanted. Once we learned that no one wanted big squashes, we tried to pick them while they were no more than eight or ten inches long, but sometimes we would miss and find we had a monster. These I would cut in half lengthwise, then scoop out the halves to make shells that I filled with a mixture of sausage, bread crumbs, and chopped tomatoes, topped with cheese, and baked.

Summer squashes are squashes that we eat when the skin is soft and tender and the seeds inside still immature, unlike winter squashes, which are consumed when the shells are hard and a cavity has formed to hold the mature seeds. As a number of different kinds of summer squash are available, it makes for versatility in the kitchen to grow a variety in the potager. I usually plant a crookneck, a round pattypan, both pale green and yellow varieties, and two or three types of zucchini, including the French Ronde de Nice, which has a particularly fine skin and delicate flavor.

Zucchini Galettes with Crème Fraîche

Grate zucchini on the large holes of a grater or a food processor. Grate a little onion and mix it in. Squeeze dry. Season with salt, pepper, and minced fresh basil. Heat some butter or oil in a skillet, then add heaping tablespoonfuls, one at a time, of the mixture. Flatten with the back of a wooden spoon or spatula and cook until browned. Turn and cook the other side until browned. Serve with dots of crème fraîche or sour cream.

The male blossoms of all summer squashes, which provide pollen but bear no fruit, are readily distinguished by their long stems. The female blossom can be identified by the swelling at its base, which if pollinated becomes the squash. Squash blossoms, either male or female, can be added to soups, stews, and salads and are also good stuffed. Françoise makes a tasty dish of squash blossoms stuffed with minced onions, garlic, bread crumbs, and ground beef, which are then put in a baking dish, covered with a fresh tomato-basil sauce, and baked.

Plant summer squashes in mounds or rows described in the section on cucumbers, and keep them well supplied with water. Summer squashes can be planted in containers at least eighteen inches in diameter and eighteen inches deep.

STUFFED SQUASH BLOSSOMS IN TOMATO COULIS

Harvest male squash blossoms early in the morning when they are fully open, and keep their stems immersed in a glass of water in the refrigerator until ready to use. If they are too tightly closed, soak the blossoms for a few minutes in ice water to reopen them. Mix together fresh goat cheese and minced roasted red pepper. Season with fresh thyme, salt, and pepper. Put a tablespoon or so of the cheese mixture into each blossom, enough to reach to the point where the petals divide. Fold the petals over, overlapping them. Place the stuffed blossoms, fold side down, in a baking dish and surround them with a sauce made of cooked-down fresh tomatoes seasoned with a little garlic, onion, salt, pepper, and fresh basil. Bake at 350 degrees F for 30 minutes, or until piping hot.

Winter Squashes

Most pumpkins and other winter squashes require a longer growing season than summer squashes do, needing anywhere from 78 to 100 days to reach maturity. That means giving up part of the potager for the entire summer. They have large leaves sometimes two feet across and long trailing vines, and it is wonderful to watch them grow and spread, especially as fall approaches and the squashes begin to color beneath their green canopy. The blossoms, like those of summer squashes, can be eaten.

Pumpkins are one of the many winter squashes, although today the bulk of the readily available varieties are not very flavorful, having been bred for early ripening and uniformity for the Halloween pumpkin market. For flavor, look for green acorn squash, Hubbard, and butternut. If you can find the seeds, the Italian Chioggia squash is one of the best baking squashes you will ever taste, along with Musquée de Provence. In both instances, the meat is dense and nutty, creamy and smooth, with a texture akin to sweet potatoes.

Plant winter squashes in mounds or rows, as for summer squashes, but the mounds must be at least three feet in diameter and the seeds planted one inch deep. Thin to no more than one plant per mound. Because these vines, especially the pumpkin, require so much space and time in the garden, try to plant them along the back or the side, where the vines have extra room to spread and won't overcome other vegetables.

Water them deeply and often in their early stages of growth. Cut water back a bit once the fruits have appeared. Continue to water deeply until the fruits are nearly full size. Then cut off the water. The fruit will fill and ripen.

It is easy to know when a squash is ready to harvest because the vines start to die back and the leaves begin to crumble into dry, scratchy heaps. Once this happens, cut the stem. Don't pull the squash from the stem because it will cause a wound where decay can start. Besides, the squashes look much better with their stems intact. Once cut, let winter squashes and pumpkins stand outside for a few days to cure, then store them in a root cellar, garage, or other cool place.

Small-size pumpkins and other winter squashes can be grown in containers that are at least eighteen inches deep and eighteen inches in diameter.

patty-pan squash

acorn squash

pumpkin

Sweet Potatoes

One day I came home from a long day in San Francisco and went out into the potager to wander around and soothe my soul. Near the fence I saw a half dozen or so bedraggled plants, all flopped over and wilted looking, stuck down into soggy, newly watered soil. I asked my husband what they were, and he told me they were sweet-potato plants that Nigel, a neighboring farmer, had brought over and had planted for me. Well, I was skeptical that those sad little things, put into the ground on a blistering-hot July day, would ever amount to anything, so they were cursorily watered throughout the summer and into fall. The vines eventually grew and spread, although not dramatically. In mid-October, when I decided to pull out the neighboring pepper plants, I thought to myself, "And now it's time to get rid of those worthless sweet-potato vines." I set about digging them up. When I lifted my shovel the first time, I was astounded to find big, beautiful sweet potatoes dangling from it! I laid them out to cure before rubbing off the dirt and storing them away to use throughout the fall and winter. Baked whole, then split open and sprinkled with salt, pepper, and a little chopped fresh parsley and crowned with a dot of butter, they are a treat throughout the winter.

A single sweet potato tuber, planted where it will receive at least three quarters of a day of full sun, will produce dozens of shoots. When ten to twelve inches long, cut off the shoots and plant them individually. Each of them will produce a pound or more of sweet potatoes. If you can acquire disease-free sweet-potato seed stock, you can produce your own shoots by planting whole tubers in April, then cutting them approximately ten weeks later. If the seed stock is unavailable, the ready-to-plant shoots can be acquired through specialty suppliers.

Plant sweet potatoes into very wet soil, and keep it moist throughout its growing season. Sweet potatoes are suitable for container plantings if the container is a least three feet deep and two feet in diameter.

Fennel and Leeks

Although fennel and leeks are not botanically related, I think of them together in the garden because I plant them at the same time and harvest them similarly, in their different stages from tiny shoots in late summer to full grown in spring. Growing up in southern California in the late fifties and early sixties, leeks and fennel were not a part of my experience, even though my mother was an adventuresome cook. The first time I saw these vegetables was at the open markets during my student days in France, but it wasn't until we moved to Haute Provence that I learned how to cook with them. Victorine taught me to prepare both leeks and fennel in gratins, napped with a béchamel sauce and topped with toasty buttered bread crumbs. I loved them both, and a number of years later when I grew my own, I was able to sample and cook with them at all their different stages.

Leeks are quite easily grown from seed. Plant them in rows or scatter-plant and cover to a depth of one-quarter inch. They need at least three-quarters of a day of full sun and should be well watered. When the seedlings are five or six inches tall, and just thick enough to pull, thin to about one inch apart. Use the leek thinnings in salads, where they impart a delicate, sweet, onionlike flavor. Later, when the leeks are about the size of a pencil, thin again, this time to two inches apart. These small leeks are the same size as the wild leeks that are gathered in early spring from Provençal vineyards for use in leeks vinaigrette or in scrambled eggs. The remaining leeks can be harvested as desired, through fall and winter. In mild-winter climates, the harvest can continue into spring when the leeks send up seed stalks and flower.

There are many leek varieties, some developed specially to be planted in summer for fall harvest, others that are very cold hardy for use in cold-winter climates, and still others to plant in spring for summer harvest. Consult mail-order seed catalogs to help you make your selection. Leeks can be grown in containers at least two feet deep and eighteen inches in diameter.

Fennel plays much the same role in the garden as leeks do because it can be used in the kitchen in all stages of growth. I scatter-plant the seeds in a sunny spot in a row in a one-inch-wide swath or in a patch, then cover them with about one-half inch of soil. They need water to germinate but are surprisingly drought resistant after that. As they grow, I thin to about one inch apart, using the youngest ones as seasonings in soups and stews, or minced to flavor salad dressings and sauces. Later, when the bulb at the base is about one inch wide, I thin again, this time to about two inches apart, and sauté the succulent young fennel or thinly slice it for salads. The remaining fennel can be harvested as desired through fall, and in mild climates through winter into spring. Where cold winters prevail, the harvest period can be extended by mulching or otherwise protecting the fennel from freezes. The mature bulbs, left too long in the ground, can become a little too fibrous to use uncooked, and are instead treated to slow braises.

The stalks that grow atop the swollen bulbs make excellent seasonings when stuffed into the cavities of fish or used as a flavoring ingredient. As the spring days lengthen, the stalks put forth buds and bright yellow blossoms, and I leave a few of these in the potager so that I can collect the seeds. The fresh seeds are pungently sweet, unlike purchased fennel seeds, and are a wonderful flavoring ingredient.

Mature bulbs have tap roots too deep for container growing. If you must grow fennel in containers, harvest it young.

Radicchio, Escarole, and Frisée

From late fall through spring, big, fat, succulent radicchio heads are obtained by planting seeds early enough in the summer so that the roots can develop and thicken sufficiently to produce the second growth that forms the red-and-white heads characteristic of the vegetable. Sow them about one inch apart, then thin to six inches apart. Transplants may be used as well, but radicchio grows easily from seed. Keep the seedlings well watered throughout their growth. The first growth is a mass of bitter, strapping dark green leaves that grow during summer into fall and are later cut back.

In my potager I plant radicchio in July, then cut the heads back in mid-September, dropping the trimmed leaves as a cover over the plants and allowing them about eight more weeks of growth. Beneath the mulch of leaves, the hidden plants continue to grow and form heads. After the frost, the covering leaves become brown and slimy but continue to insulate the radicchio. I never fail to be amazed when I peel away that decayed hood to discover the brightly colored, pristine leaves beneath. I have also seen radicchio growing beneath a thick mulch of straw.

Radicchio, like leeks and fennel, can be harvested over winter and into spring in areas with mild-winter climates. With adequate mulching, they can be harvested in cold-winter climates as well. Either whole heads can be cut, or in a version of the cut-and-come-again method, the hearts only can be cut out above the crown and the inner leaves will regrow. This third growth doesn't form a tight head, but rather a collection of loose leaves, ideal for salads.

Although some radicchio hybrids developed primarily for commercial plantings have a higher degree of uniformity than such open-pollinated varieties as Rouge de Verone and Palla Rosso, the open-pollinated ones are well suited to the home garden. Just don't expect tight, firm red heads. Container planting should be avoided, however, because of deep tap roots.

Escarole and frisée don't need the same amount of time to produce a second growth, so these can be planted a little later than the radicchio, in early to mid-August. As explained in the Spring chapter (page 51), these can be scatter-planted and then thinned to about four inches apart, to encourage the plants to self-blanch. Like radicchio, they can be harvested throughout fall into winter and spring in mild-winter climates, cutting out the blanched hearts and letting them regrow and cutting them again and again. In areas with cold-winter climates, the harvest can be extended somewhat by mulching.

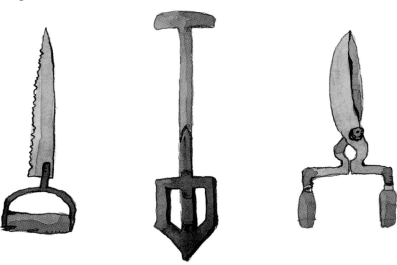

Broccoli, Cauliflower, and Cabbage

At my house, we have become spoiled by home-grown broccoli, cauliflower, and cabbage, all of which have a fresh, sweet taste that is quite different from their supermarket counterparts. These seeds can be sown in rows in late July or early August in a section of the garden that gets some shade during the hot days of summer. Sow the seeds two or three inches apart, then thin to a foot apart for cabbage and eight inches apart for broccoli and cauliflower. The thinnings can then be transplanted elsewhere into the garden. They can be stored in the refrigerator and wrapped in wet paper towels for a week or so, allowing ample time to open another section of the garden and plant them.

Unfortunately, the *Brassica* genus, and this includes our trio, are beloved by both aphids and cabbage looper moths. Cabbage loopers cut huge holes into the leaves, greatly reducing the surface area necessary for photosynthesis. Aphids can quickly cover leaves and heads with a grayish white mass of bodies and suck the sap from the plant. Fortunately, the looper larvae, whose feeding does the leaf damage, are susceptible to applications of organic Bt, a bacillus that attacks the gut of worms and nothing else. If you are vigilant and spot the first aphids, they can be controlled by washing them off or by spraying soap solutions.

When the broccoli begins to head, the growth is apparent first in the center of the plant, and eventually a short stalk will rise, topped with a tightly budded head. When this head matures and is cut, side shoots will appear where the leaves meet the stems. Although these later heads will never grow to the size of the central stalk, they are every bit as flavorful. The chartreuse Romanesco broccoli, which forms conical heads of swirled turrets of buds, only occasionally produces side shoots, but it is well worth growing for its color, texture, and mild flavor.

Once the white curds of the head have begun to develop, cauliflower, unlike broccoli, needs a little assistance in the garden. If the curds are exposed to the sunlight, they turn from snowy white to yellow. This only slightly affects the flavor but makes for a less-appealing appearance. A number of varieties are labeled self-blanching, which means they have been bred to produce leaves that wrap around the developing head and protect it from the sun. To blanch open-pollinated varieties in the old-fashioned way (as well as self-blanching types that don't always do what they are supposed to), tie the leaves around the head. Occasionally side shoots develop, but these are not noteworthy.

Cabbages, once in the garden and growing, just keep growing and growing, putting out first large outer leaves, then developing small overlaying leaves inside, continuing the process until a tight, firm head has materialized, which one can cut anytime from late fall until spring. There are a number of different cabbage varieties, in three basic shapes: the round, flat

drumhead, the pointed or conical, and the classic ball. The leaf color may be reddish purple or light or dark green. The red cabbages tend to have slightly tougher leaves than those of the green. The varieties with leaves that are crinkly and puffed like little quilts are called Savoy. In general the flavor of a Savoy is slighter milder than that of the others. Once any cabbage is cut, the remaining base of the plant will put forth new leaves, most typically in spring. In England, these "spring greens," as they are called, are considered a treat, although in my garden it is no choice between the cabbage leaves and the young spring lettuces.

Cabbages, cauliflowers, and broccolis are not particularly practical for planting in containers because of their large size and the relatively small yield per plant.

Turnips and Carrots

Turnips and carrots, which are planted in spring as well (page 47 and 54), are planted again in late August. A good location for them is beneath the now-large leaves of the eggplants. By the time the seedlings have reached six to eight inches, it will be time to start pulling out some of the eggplants, thus giving the turnips and carrots the light and space they need to continue growing.

I find that by judicious pulling of the young turnips, I am, in fact, thinning to produce large turnips that will survive in my garden deep into winter. They will be used to make delectable slow-cooked gratins, wrapped in béchamel sauce and flavored with anchovies and buttered bread crumbs.

Summer to Fall

IN NORTHERN CALIFORNIA, SUMMER OFTEN SEEMS UNENDING, WITH HOT, dry days continuing through September and deep into October. Looking at the potager bedecked with brilliant tomatoes, peppers, eggplants, and ripening winter squashes and pumpkins, it is hard to believe that all this will soon end, to be replaced by fall and winter's broccoli, cauliflower, cabbage, and greens, all planted in late summer and now growing side by side. Even as we still regale ourselves with summer's plantings of fresh shelling beans, green beans, and melons, and continue to eat outside in the warm evenings as we did in July and August, fall's inexorable arrival can be seen in the changing slant of light in the late afternoon, and in the slight drying of the tomato, melon, and cucumber vines and the crinkling edges of their leaves, even though their fruits continue to ripen. The shelling beans are plump and ready to harvest, but soon these plants will wither and the beans harden.

Activities in fall's potager are weighted on the harvesting side, because with few exceptions, its crops were actually planted in summer in order to allow enough growing time to come to maturity before the onset of winter. With the last harvests of the beans, melons, and cucumbers, their space is turned and planted to radish, tat-soi, lettuces, and spinach, all leafy, quick-growing vegetables, the same ones planted in early spring.

If you missed planting for fall during the summer (or just couldn't make yourself start taking out some of summer's vegetables), you can still, in early fall, transplant cabbage, broccoli, and cauliflower seedlings and sow turnip and carrot seeds, although the latter may not reach full size before cold temperatures shut down their growth until spring.

Vegetables planted later in fall may reach only their vegetative stage by the time the cold temperatures arrive, and will grow no more until the weather warms and the days lengthen, which is good for peas and favas. In areas with mild winters, fava beans, which thrive in cool weather, are best planted in late fall for spring harvest. That way they are given a head start that allows them enough time to flower and set pods before rising temperatures halt pollination. In areas with cold-winter climates, fava beans can be planted in early spring at the same time as peas.

Once the weather has cooled a bit and Indian summer is over, the potager offers young escarole and frisée. The cabbages and radicchios are beginning to head, and the young lettuces are ready for their first picking, along with baby fennel and leeks.

Fall

FALL IS, WITHOUT QUESTION, MY FAVORITE TIME OF THE YEAR. TO ME the new year begins then, full of hope and promise, symbolized by the potager. At no other time does the potager seem more plentiful, more varied, more lush, more full of culinary possibilities. The coming of fall strikes some primeval remnant of a cultural consciousness that awakens in me the desire for harvest, storage, snuggling down, and withdrawing from the world. The shortening days increase the dark hours, which seem better for staying in and cooking, building cozy fires, and sewing and writing, unlike summer's days, which demand being outside and active.

In a brief window of time, from September to mid-October, all of summer's bounty is at its prime, yet at the same time fall's singular vegetables and fruits, the winter squashes, shelling beans, quinces, pomegranates, and persimmons, are also ready to pick, as well as the greens and roots of fall, the same as those of spring: frisée, escarole, lettuces, carrots, and radishes. When the time window closes, summer's tomatoes, eggplants, squashes, melons, beans, and cucumbers are gone, and the potager is resplendent with hearty greens, chicories, cabbages, broccoli, cauliflower, leeks, and fennel.

ARTICHOKES

STRAWBERRIES

LETTUCE LETTUCE

LETTUCE LETTUCE

RADISH TAT-SOI ARUGULA

WINTER SQUASH

FENNEL

LEEKS

ESCAROLE RADICCHIO FRISEE

PUMPKINS

EGGPLANT

EGGPLANT

ONIONS

TURNIP

CARROTS

CHILIES

BASIL

FAVA BEANS

CILANTRO

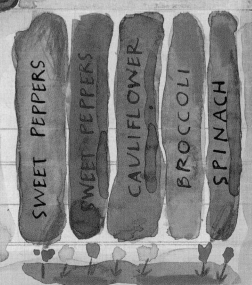

SWEET PEPPERS

SWEET PEPPERS

CAULIFLOWER

BROCCOLI

SPINACH

Although I cling to the tomatoes and peppers of summer as long as possible, other parts of the summer garden go early to create room for fall's plantings. The green beans exit to make way for the broccoli and cauliflower

BORLOTTO BEANS AND
GRILLED RADICCHIO
WITH ORECCHIETTE

Cook fresh borlotto or other meaty shelling beans in salted water for 10 to 15 minutes, or until tender to the bite. Drain and set aside. Cut a head of radicchio into thin slices; toss with olive oil, salt, and pepper. Place in a grilling basket and grill over coals. Remove when the slices are brown and the edges are crisp. While the radicchio and beans are cooking, cook the orecchiette in boiled salted water until al dente. Drain. Combine the beans, grilled radicchio, and pasta with a little olive oil, salt, pepper, and fresh thyme. Toss well. Top with grated Parmesan cheese.

seedlings. The early green beans were finished in August, and now the rest are uprooted, their bamboo teepees pulled down, and the soil rototilled and raked. In their place go lettuces. As soon as the last of the shelling beans are harvested, I'll plant spinach in their rows.

Where the sweet potatoes were recently dug, I plant a row or two of fava beans into the freshly prepared ground. Cucumber and melon vines are cut and pulled and their ground, once turned and raked, is sown with seeds of winter greens and radishes. Slowly, the garden is being transformed from summer to fall. Soon, when the temperature drops and the eggplants and tomatoes no longer flower, the plants are removed and part of their space planted to fava beans. The rest will be reserved for December plantings of garlic and onions. When the last of the winter squashes have matured and they have been picked and stored and the area cleared, prepared, and planted to the last lettuces, the transformation of the potager from summer to fall is complete.

Arugula, Tat-soi, and Radishes

These cool weather standbys are planted just as they were months ago in spring (page 42). As I sow their seeds in part of the patch so recently occupied by melons, I find I am now anxious for the crisp bite of the radish, the strong, hearty taste of the tat-soi leaves, and the peppery edge of the arugula. These look especially appetizing when scatter-planted next to one another, so that when they come up they make a solid sheet of color. As always, the radishes are first to appear and their light green leaves give a fresh, spring-like cast to the garden, followed soon by the arugula and tat-soi leaves. If we have a late-September heat wave, as we often do, I'll need to make sure these plants get extra water to keep them from becoming too pungent. In cold-weather climates, though, this won't be a problem.

Lettuces

As in spring, lettuces are central to the garden (page 48). I like to plant them in early September so they will grow to nearly full size during the mild days of October. If you live in a climate with an early winter, move up the planting date to August for a fall harvest. Once the weather turns cold in November, the lettuces stop growing. Mild-winter climates are more forgiving, of course, and the lettuces will keep along with the radicchio, escarole, and frisée planted in late summer, and can be cut in spring.

Put in as many different kinds as possible to keep the kitchen well supplied with a variety of colors, tastes, and textures. If your planting is timely, you will find you have tender, young lettuces to mix with sweet red and yellow cherry tomatoes and snippets of basil for a crossover-season salad. The dressing must be light, as a vinaigrette of fruity oil and aromatic vinegar is too heavy for these tender leaves.

Spinach

Spinach is an important part of the fall planting, just as it is of the spring (page 54). A four-by-five-foot patch, generously scatter-planted, will serve a kitchen's needs until midwinter in a mild climate if the leaves are cut rather than the entire plant pulled. It takes a full colander of spinach leaves to make enough for one serving of steamed spinach per person, so an abundant planting is necessary.

Not only does spinach make an excellent salad green, but it seems to go well with the season's slowly cooked braises, stews, and soups. Once I served quickly sautéed spinach leaves dressed with no more than a squeeze of lemon juice, salt, and pepper to accompany a crown roast of pork at a formal November dinner party. The spinach came bright green and sizzling hot from the stove directly to the table and was served on everyone's plate immediately. It was the hit of the meal.

SAUTÉED SPINACH AND CHANTERELLE MUSHROOMS

Heat a little olive oil in a skillet and add some minced garlic. Sauté for 2 or 3 minutes, then add chanterelles or other mushrooms, whole if small or halved or quartered if large, and sauté for another 2 or 3 minutes. Season with salt and pepper and minced fresh parsley; set aside. Rinse the spinach in cold water. Drain but do not dry. Heat a little olive oil in a wok or skillet and add some minced garlic. Sauté for 2 or 3 minutes, then add the spinach. Cover with a lid and let cook for 2 or 3 minutes, or until the spinach is wilted but still bright green. Add the mushrooms and their juices, mix together, and serve.

Fava Beans

My earliest memory of fava beans is from the rabbity house in France where my first husband and I lived when our son, Oliver, was born. He was just a few months old and quite the talk of the village because he was only the second baby to be born there in over five years. We had lots of villagers coming by to see him and to bring him little gifts. One evening late in spring there was a knock on the door. It was one of the local farmers, M. Embark. Short, burly, with curly dark hair graying on the edges, he was a familiar sight in our area because he farmed land at both the beginning of our road and its end. He handed me a fistful of pods and asked if I had ever cooked them. I said no. He peeled one open and showed me the tiny beans inside, no larger than the tip of my little finger. I had been busy fixing dinner when he arrived, and he asked if I wanted him to show me how to cook them. I said yes, so he stepped up to the tiny two-burner stove, picked up a small skillet, and poured in a little olive oil from the bottle I kept on a shelf nearby. We popped the beans from their pods and put them in the skillet. He cooked them for a few minutes, stirring them with a wooden spoon. He plucked some dried thyme from the bunch I had tied on the beam above and sprinkled the leaves over the beans. Kissing his fingertips in a typically French gesture, he said now I had a delicious *fricot* for dinner, and anytime I wanted more *fèves*, just wave him down on the road. And, could he see the new baby?

So, each fall when I plant fava beans, I think of M. Embark and of my first taste of these wonderful meaty beans that I have eaten so many times since with so much pleasure. Unlike green beans and shelling beans, which are members of the New World *Phaseolus* genus, fava beans, of the *Vicia* genus, belong not to the New World but to the Old. Remnants of them have been found in the tombs of Egyptian pharaohs and in archaeological excavations of the prehistoric Swiss lake dwellers. The bean seeds are large, the size of a thumb tip, and must be planted deep, one and a half to two inches down, and spaced six inches apart.

In a mild-winter climate, sow the beans in fall. Ideally, the plants will be six to eight inches tall before they stop growing from the onset of cold weather. Once the warmer, lengthening days of spring arrive, the plants will grow rapidly, bursting forth with black-throated white blossoms followed by the apple green pods. The pods will often grow eight to ten inches long, with one pod carrying six to seven beans. If the pods are only six to seven inches long, the beans will be tiny, like the ones M. Embark first gave me, and can be eaten either cooked or raw. As they begin to get larger, they are best cooked, either with or without the outer skin.

Many Europeans cook them at home with the skins on, but in the United States they seem to be more often prepared with the skins removed, especially in restaurants. The skin, which turns brownish on cooking, is slightly bitter, which Mediterranean people tell me is exactly what they like about these beans. Peeling them is not difficult, and the easiest method is to drop the beans in boiling water for thirty seconds, then put them into a sieve and run cold water over them. Using your thumbnail or the tip of a knife, slit the skin. Peel away the skin or squeeze the bean between your thumb and index finger so it pops out of its skin, often in halves. It takes about two pounds of fava pods to make two cups of shelled beans. If skinned, the same amount will yield about one cup.

FAVA BEANS
SAUTÉED WITH GARLIC

Heat a little olive oil in a skillet and add minced garlic and minced onion. Sauté for 2 or 3 minutes, then add young, still-tender shelled fava beans. Sprinkle with fresh thyme leaves. Cook, stirring, over medium heat for 4 or 5 minutes, then reduce the heat and continue for another 5 or 6 minutes, or until the favas are cooked through and soft and some of the skins are split. Season with salt and pepper.

Fall to Winter

WINTER, LIKE SPRING, MAKES A SUDDEN APPEARANCE AT MY HOUSE. While I'm still enjoying the warm days and cool evenings of fall, the colors turning on the grape leaves, and the thinning sun, the air turns cold without warning, the sky goes gray and rain begins to fall. Not a gentle shower, but a bone-piercing-cold winter-storm downpour that soaks the ground through, whips the leaves from the vines and the trees, and keeps us snuggled inside the house, with a fire burning and stove-top stews.

The cold signals the definitive end of fall in the potager, the completed transition from the autumnal mix of tomatoes, eggplants, summer and winter squashes, beans, and greens to winter's hardy population of cabbages, broccoli, cauliflower, leeks, chicories, and greens, all planted in late summer or early fall. From November until spring, these will be the flavors of the season's kitchen, along with the stored winter squashes, sweet potatoes, and dried beans.

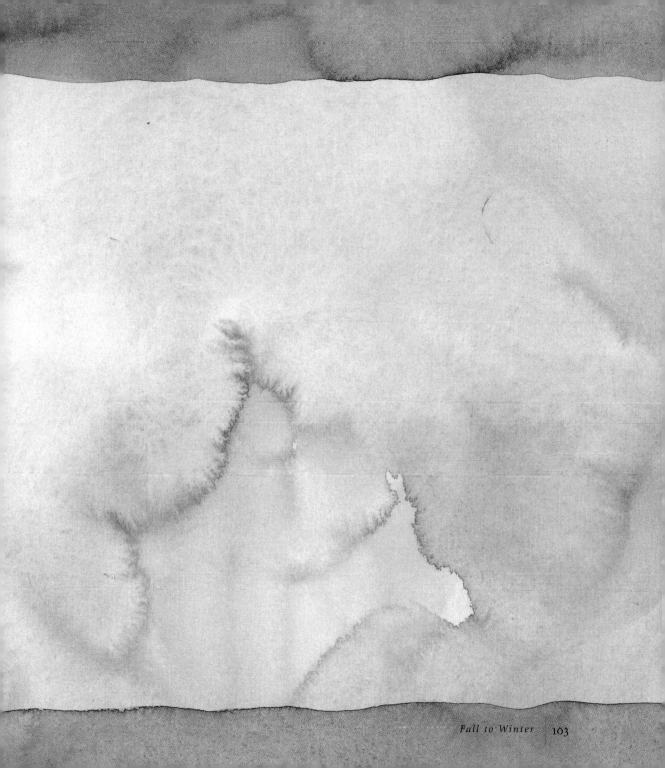

Winter

THE POTAGER, IF WELL PLANNED, IS FULL OF A VARIETY OF VEGETABLES TO eat over the winter, especially in areas with mild-winter climates. Most of the crops have been planted in late summer, and some in early fall. Few vegetables will be planted in winter for several reasons. Some seeds won't germinate because of the low soil temperatures, and those that will germinate won't grow much past seedling stage until the weather warms again in spring. Transplanted seedlings don't evidence much growth either. They simply wait until the weather changes before they start putting down new roots and sending forth tender shoots. Finally, it is unrewarding to try to garden in cold mud. In my area, the coldest times are January and early February. December has some cold and rainy days, but for the most part it tends to be sunny and rather mild. Rarely is it cold and rainy enough on Christmas Day to stay inside or even to bundle up outside.

November and December are fine planting times for onion and garlic sets in mild-winter climates. Elsewhere they are set out in spring or early summer. The sets look like the garlic heads and pearl onions that you purchase in markets, but they have been grown from certified disease-free seed.

I have also found lettuce and arugula to yield a successful March and April harvest when planted in December. But my problem is the birds, which come to overwinter in the shrub roses and make forays into the garden,

ARTICHOKES

STRAWBERRIES

LETTUCE

LETTUCE

LETTUCE

LETTUCE

LETTUCE

LETTUCE

BROCCOLI

FENNEL

LEEKS

CAULIFLOWER

ESCAROLE　RADICCHIO　FRISEE

ONION

ONION

TURNIP

CARROT

GARLIC

GARLIC

FAVA BEANS

FAVA BEANS

CABBAGE--- GREEN SAVOY

CABBAGE--- RED

CAULIFLOWER

BROCCOLI

SPINACH

devastating young seedlings and pecking away at the established plants. Even the knowledge that my winged enemies may win the battle of winter's potager doesn't stop me from planting lettuces, though, and I make every effort to protect them. Garlic and onions, fortunately, are among the few vegetables they leave alone.

Onions

I disregard the suggested planting distances on packets and in vegetable manuals because I don't want to grow onions for an all-at-once harvest. I prefer to have the vegetables available to cook at every stage whenever possible. So, instead of the recommended six to eight inches apart for onions, I plant the sets literally touching one another at a depth of two inches, in either a row or a patch in a space that has at least a half day of sun. If the rains

don't keep them well watered, I do, as they need water for the bulbs to develop.

Four or five weeks after planting, thin whippets of chivelike green onions are ready to bring into the kitchen. This means you can have fresh onion greens in the kitchen, and because of judicious pulling, the proper space separating the plants in the garden to produce full-size onions in spring. By late February and early March, the green onions have grown to one-half inch or more and have begun swelling at the base. They are pulled day by day and used in salads, stews, savory puddings, and breads, as well as to season all kinds of dishes from pasta sauce to curry. The space between the plants will continue to increase until late March and early April, when the remaining onions are the size of softballs, perfect for slicing and grilling. They will have gotten so large they are breaking surrounding soil, bursting forth from the ground, their tops now nearly all dry, the signal that they are mature and ready to harvest. A few continue to grow and send up a seed stalk, and these I leave in the garden until they flower, the stalks now two or three feet long. I use the flowers to season the first of spring's pea soups, or simply put them in a vase and enjoy their beauty.

Garlic

The gardener separates garlic sets into cloves to plant. Each clove will in turn produce a whole head of garlic. I treat the individual cloves much like I do the onion sets, planting them two inches deep and closer together than recommended, because I like to pull some of the young green garlic to use in the winter and spring kitchens. The heads will not ripen and mature until early summer. They need at least a half day of sun, and if the rain doesn't supply enough water, they need regular watering, but not to the point of sogginess.

I do leave more space between these than I do between the onions sets. The base needs to be at least an inch wide for enough flavor to have developed to make it worthwhile to pull. So the cloves, still in their papery covering, are spaced about one and one-half inches apart and planted two inches deep.

Plant onion and garlic in containers eighteen inches deep and twelve inches apart. Container growing is not ideal unless bulbs are harvested young.

Once the planted cloves have produced stalks and somewhat substantial bases, they can be pulled and treated much like the green onions they resemble. Pulling every other one over a period of time will allow increased space between the remaining garlic to allow for the development of the bulbous base.

The young bulbs, pulled when about the size of a walnut and before the membranes form that separate the individual cloves, are a wonderful spring

BRAISED FENNEL
WITH TOMATOES AND
GARLIC CRUMBS

Cut fennel bulbs lengthwise into ¼-inch-thick slices. Sauté them in olive oil until they begin to turn golden. Add 1 or 2 canned plum tomatoes, chopped, and continue to cook until the tomato is slightly reduced. Place in a shallow baking dish and sprinkle the top with a mixture of toasted bread crumbs, chopped parsley, minced garlic, and minced lemon zest. Drizzle the surface with olive oil. Bake at 350 degrees F until bubbling hot and the top is golden.

delicacy. They can be cooked whole slowly in the oven in a covered baking dish along with peas or favas and a little butter and olive oil, or sautéed and served whole, as one would tiny onions. The garlic that remains in the garden into late spring will begin to develop cloves, which I use as I would dried garlic, separating the cloves before cooking with them. Finally, the last of the garlic is allowed to mature. When the tops start drying and turning brown, I dig them and put them in a dry place to cure for several days before tying them into bunches and hanging one in the kitchen and the others in the cellar.

Lettuces

If the ground is not soggy from rains, I plant a mixture of lettuces in December or January, and these give me a head start in spring (see page 48). I'll have tender lettuces by mid to late March.

Winter Squashes, Sweet Potatoes, Fennel, Leeks, Radicchio, Escarole, Frisée, Broccoli, Cauliflower, Cabbage, Turnips

If you planted well in the summer for the above winter bounty (see page 82), you should be happily reaping the rewards. The following recipes feature the earthy delights of your summer toil and the rich flavors of your winter harvest.

BROCCOLI AND ANCHOVY PASTA

Steam small florets of broccoli. Make a paste of anchovy fillets, garlic, and olive oil. Cook pasta such as orecchiette or penne. Drain and add butter and pepper, the anchovy paste, and the broccoli. Sprinkle with red pepper flakes, if desired.

SAVORY WINTER SQUASH

Cut winter squashes into halves, remove and discard the seeds and fibers, and place cut side down on a buttered baking sheet. Bake at 350 degrees F for 1 to 2 hours, or until tender; the timing depends upon size. Scoop out the soft, creamy flesh and whip with minced fresh sage, salt, pepper, and butter.

Savoy Cabbage, Onions, Potatoes, and Corned Beef

Prepare purchased corn beef as directed on the package. It will need 2 to 4 hours to cook, depending upon the weight. Remove the large outer leaves of the cabbage and cut the head through the core into quarters or sixths, depending upon the size. Peel several onions, leaving the root bases intact. Cut the onions through the stem ends into quarters. Scrub potatoes and cut them lengthwise into halves or quarters, depending upon their size. Bring a large pan of salted water to a boil, add the onions and potatoes, and cook for about 15 minutes. Add the cabbage and cook for another 10 minutes, or just until the cabbage is limp and tender. Set aside and keep warm. When the corned beef is done, cut it into thin slices and serve with the drained vegetables, drizzling a little of the cooking liquid from the corned beef over them.

Curried Cauliflower with Toasted Walnuts

Melt a nubbin butter in a skillet, then add chopped onion and garlic, carrot slices, and green apple cubes. Sauté for several minutes, then sprinkle with flour, turmeric, cumin, red pepper flakes, and a little salt and stir to coat all the ingredients and to brown them a bit. Add a little chicken broth to form a sauce and stir to blend. Add a few currants, cover, and cook for about 10 minutes over low heat. Meanwhile, steam cauliflower florets. Add these to the sauce and re-cover. Cook for another 10 minutes. Uncover, raise the heat to high, and cook for another few minutes to reduce slightly. Sprinkle with toasted walnuts and serve with rice, chutney, and plain yogurt.

Savory Sweet Potato Pudding

Steam sliced sweet potatoes for almost 10 minutes, or until just barely tender. Set aside. Soak slices of day-old bread in milk until soft, then squeeze the milk from the bread. Butter a baking dish and make a layer of the squeezed bread. Sprinkle with minced fresh oregano or marjoram, a little salt and pepper, and top with a layer of sweet potatoes followed by a layer of Teleme or other soft cheese. Repeat, ending with a layer of bread. Pour over all about a cup of milk mixed with an egg and seasoned with salt and pepper; the layers should be well moistened but not floating. Dot with butter. Bake at 350 degrees F for 35 to 45 minutes, or until the top is browned and a knife inserted into the center comes out clean.

Gratin of Leeks with Prosciutto

Slit the whites of leeks nearly through lengthwise, then steam. When done, wrap 2 or 3 leeks, depending upon size, with a thin slice of prosciutto to make a bundle. Lay the bundles in a buttered baking dish and make a sauce by heating ½ cup milk to almost boiling, then stirring in 4 ounces fresh goat cheese and a sprinkling of salt, pepper, and fresh thyme. Stir until the cheese dissolves and the sauce thickens. Pour over the leek bundles, top with toasted bread crumbs, and dot with butter. Bake at 425 degrees F until heated through, the sauce bubbles, and the topping is browned.

Escarole, Gruyère, and Bacon Salad

Tear escarole leaves into pieces and put them in a bowl. Cut Canadian bacon or pancetta into ½-inch cubes and cook in a skillet until browned. Remove and set aside to drain. Let the fat in the pan cool, then pour off all but about 1 tablespoon. Add olive oil and red wine vinegar or balsamic vinegar to the pan as needed to make enough vinaigrette for the salad. Season with pepper. Cook over low heat just enough to warm the vinaigrette. Pour it over the escarole and turn. Add ½-inch cubes of Gruyère cheese and most of the bacon and mix together. Serve on salad plates and garnish with the remaining bacon.

Cauliflower with Gorgonzola Sauce

Steam a head of cauliflower. Make a béchamel sauce, and when it is done, stir in chunks of Gorgonzola cheese. Place the cauliflower in a shallow bowl and pour the sauce over it.

Coleslaw with Avocado, Chicken, and Meyer Lemon Dressing

Combine 2 cups grated cabbage, 2 cups chopped cooked chicken breast, ¼ cup chopped fresh parsley, and salt and pepper to taste. Add a vinaigrette made with olive oil and Meyer lemon juice, then gently fold in cubes of avocado.

CONCLUSION

EACH YEAR MY POTAGER HAS ITS SUCCESSES AND ITS FAILURES, AND each year I learn something new about the connection between the earth, the food it produces, and myself. The discoveries are often small ones, like finding a blanket of tiny parsley seedlings beneath the failing hollyhock. Soon I become excited by the thought of having a far greater abundance of the aromatic herb than I would have ever planted, and I see myself using it with abandon throughout the spring. Sometimes nature's lessons are less rewarding. An invasion of hungry pests can go unnoticed in a thick, beautiful bed of radicchio until it is too late, and turn the plants to lace overnight. I have watched with dismay as days and days of autumn rain transform the freshly tilled sections of my potager into knee-high, boot-sucking mud soup, conscious that I won't get it planted in time for winter after all and knowing that the clumpy bare earth will rebuke me for months.

Above all, season after season, year after year, the potager remains a patch of soil where anything can happen, where I, in partnership with the earth, the sun, and water, can create a place in which vegetables, herbs, and fruits flourish for me to gather. From my harvest I can make soups, salads, quiches, crêpes, breads, gratins, and stir-fries, all fashioned with my own hands. It is an exhilarating and liberating sense of power always tempered, of course, by the power of nature, the partner I can't forget. Nevertheless, each day a heady feeling of possibility accompanies me into the potager and kitchen, a feeling that has never diminished. That spirit of possibility is the secret joy of a potager.

Sources

JOHHNY'S SELECTED SEEDS
310 Foss Hill Road
Albion, ME 04910
(207) 437-9294
Offers a wide selection of
vegetable seeds of all kinds,
with a particular focus on
short-season vegetables for
areas with cold winter
climates. Free catalog.

PINETREE GARDEN SEEDS
Route 100
New Gloucester, ME 04260
(207) 926-3400
Many unusual seeds, includ-
ing 45 different varieties of
tomato seeds. Free catalog.

SEEDS OF CHANGE
1364 Rufina Circle #5
Santa Fe, NM 87501
(505) 438-8080
Organic vegetable seeds
including many varieties of
hybrid and heirlooms, plus
seed potatoes, garlic, and
herbs. Free catalog.

THE COOK'S GARDEN
P.O. Box 535
Londonderry, VT 05148
(800) 457-9703
Fax (800) 457-9705

SOUTHERN EXPOSURE SEED
EXCHANGE
P.O. Box 170
Earlyville, VA 22936
(804) 973-4703
Fax (804) 973-8717
An extensive selection of garlic
and onion sets, heirloom and
unusual tomato, sweet pepper,
chili pepper, beans, and corn,
as well as many other vegeta-
bles. Catalog costs $3.00.

SHEPHERD'S GARDEN SEEDS
30 Irene Street
Torrington, CT 06790-6658
(860) 482-3638
Fax (860) 482-0532
A flower and a vegetable
catalog, with over half the
offerings being vegetables
and herbs, including garlic
and onion sets and seed
potatoes.

THOMPSON & MORGAN
P.O. Box 1308
Jackson, NJ 08527-0308
(908) 363-2225
Fax (908) 363-9356
Primarily flower seeds,
including many unusal
flowers, but also a good
selection of European
vegetables, illustrated with
full-color photographs. Free
catalog.

GARDEN SEED INVENTORY:
An Inventory of Seed Catalogs
Listing All Garden Seed
Varieties.
Edited by Kent Whealy.
Available by mail order in
the United States.
Seed Saver Publications
Rural Route 3, Box 239
Decorah, IA 52101
Write to inquire for price
and shipping charges.
Lists hundreds of vegetables
followed by descriptions
of their appearance, taste,
growth habits, and other
relevant information.
Includes a list of mail-order
seed companies.

FRUIT, BERRY, AND NUT INVENTORY: *An Inventory of Nursery Catalogs Listing All Fruit, Berry, and Nut Varieties.*
Edited by Kent Whealy.
Available by mail order in the United States.
Seed Saver Publications
Rural Route 3, Box 239
Decorah, IA 52101
Write to inquire for price and shipping charges.
Lists varieties of fruits, nuts, and berries followed by descriptions of their color, taste, texture, growth habits, hardiness, and other relevant information. Includes a list of mail-order nurseries.

THE NATURAL GARDENING COMPANY
217 San Anselmo Avenue
San Anselmo, CA 94960
(707) 766-9303
Fax (707) 766-9747
A fine selection of organic garden products, including fertilizers and soil amendments. Free catalog.

PEACEFUL VALLEY FARM SUPPLY
P.O. Box 2209
Grass Valley, CA 94945
(916) 272-4769
Fax (916) 272-4794
A leader in supply products and consulting services for organic farmers throughout the United States. Catalog includes organic fertilizers, soil amendments, seeds, bulbs, onion and garlic sets, potato seeds, and many other products. Catalog costs $2.00.

HARMONY FARM SUPPLY
Warehouse Store
3244 Gravenstein Highway North
Sebastopol, CA 95472
P.O. Box 460
Graton, CA 95444
(707) 923-9125
Fax (707) 823-1734
A wide selection of organic products and books, plus bare-root fruit trees in season. Catalog costs $2.00.

Index